Catholics and Evangelicals for the Common Good

Catholics and Evangelicals for the Common Good

A Dialogue in an Historic Convergence

EDITED BY

Ronald J. Sider and John Borelli

CASCADE *Books* · Eugene, Oregon

Cascade Books
An Imprint of Wipf and Stock Publishers
199 W. 8th Ave., Suite 3
Eugene, OR 97401

www.wipfandstock.com

PAPERBACK ISBN: 978-1-5326-1220-6
HARDCOVER ISBN: 978-1-5326-1222-0
EBOOK ISBN: 978-1-5326-1221-3

Cataloguing-in-Publication data:

Names: Sider, Ronald J., editor. | Borelli, John, editor.

Title: Catholics and evangelicals for the common good : a dialogue in an historic convergence / Ronald J. Sider and John Borelli, editors.

Description: Eugene, OR: Cascade Books, 2018 | Includes bibliographical references.

Identifiers: ISBN 978-1-5326-1220-6 (paperback) | ISBN 978-1-5326-1222-0 (hardcover) | ISBN 978-1-5326-1221-3 (ebook)

Subjects: LCSH: Catholic Church—Relations—Evangelicalism. | Evangelicalism—Relations—Catholic Church. | Mission of the church.

Classification: BR1641.C37 C39 2018 (print) | BR1641 (ebook)

Manufactured in the U.S.A.   OCTOBER 31, 2018

Table of Contents

Contributors vii

Introduction xi
John Borelli and Ronald J. Sider

PART ONE: FROM HOSTILITY TO COOPERATION

Chapter 1. A Brief History of Modern Evangelical
Social Engagement in America 3
John Fea

Chapter 2. Evangelical-Catholic Cooperation in Public Policy 17
Galen Carey

Chapter 3. Reflections on Catholics and Evangelicals in Public Life:
History and Mission, Assets and Lessons, Directions and Dangers 20
John Carr

Chapter 4. Lessons to Be Learned from the Political Engagement of
Evangelicals and Catholics: An Evangelical Perspective 35
Stephen V. Monsma

Chapter 5. Forming Consciences for Faithful Citizenship: Underlying
Philosophical, Theological, and Methodological Premises 48
John Borelli

Table of Contents

PART TWO: IMMIGRATION, RACISM, THE
SANCTITY OF HUMAN LIFE, AND PEACE

Chapter 6. Immigration: A Survey of Biblical Teaching
in Evangelical Perspective 69
M. Daniel Carroll R.

Chapter 7. What Is God's Dream? Reflections on Solidarity with Refugees
and Displaced Persons 87
Leo J. O'Donovan, SJ

Chapter 8. Racial Reconciliation and the Pro-Life Agenda:
An African American Perspective 99
Cheryl J. Sanders

Chapter 9. Honoring the Sacredness of Life in Public:
An Evangelical Reflection 108
David P. Gushee

Chapter 10. Theological Perspectives on Nuclear Disarmament
and Development 119
Drew Christiansen, SJ

PART THREE: THE COMMON GOOD AS COMMON
GROUND

Chapter 11. Catholic and Evangelical Support
for the Common Good and Human Rights 131
Glen Harold Stassen

Chapter 12. Morality, Government, and the Common Good:
Understanding How Coercive Power Operates in Our Daily Lives 153
Daniel Finn

Chapter 13. A Vision for Major, Sustained Catholic-Evangelical
Partnership on Public Policy 160
Ronald J. Sider

List of Contributors

John Borelli is Special Assistant for Catholic Identity and Dialogue to the President of Georgetown University, a position he has held since 2004. He served sixteen years at the Secretariat for Ecumenical and Interreligious Affairs, United States Conference of Catholic Bishops, and was a consultor to the Vatican's Pontifical Council for Interreligious Dialogue for seventeen years. He holds a doctorate in history of religions and theology from Fordham University and has written extensively in theology, history of religions, ecumenism, and interreligious relations.

Galen Carey is Vice President for Government Relations at the National Association of Evangelicals. He and his wife Delia previously served for more than twenty-five years with World Relief, the humanitarian arm of the NAE. He earned his Master of Divinity at Trinity Evangelical Divinity School and his Doctor of Ministry at McCormick Theological Seminary. He is the coauthor, with Leith Anderson, of *Faith in the Voting Booth: Practical Wisdom for Voting Well.*

John Carr is the founder and Director of the Initiative on Catholic Social Thought and Public Life at Georgetown University. He served for more than two decades as Director of the Department of Justice, Peace and Human Development of the United States Conference of Catholic Bishops.

M. Daniel Carroll R. (Rodas) is Blanchard Professor of Old Testament at Wheaton College and Graduate School. His areas of research are Old Testament social ethics and the prophetic literature. Dr. Carroll is half-Guatemalan and has been involved with Hispanic immigrant communities for many years. He has written extensively on the Bible and immigration, including *Christians at the Border: Immigration, the Church, and the Bible,* which is now in a second edition.

Drew Christiansen, SJ, is Distinguished Professor of Ethics and Global Development at Georgetown University and Senior Research Fellow at the university's Berkley Center for Religion, Ethics and World Affairs. Previously he served as director of the United States Conference of Catholic Bishops' Office of International Justice and Peace and president and editor in chief of *America*. He is serving his second term with the US Methodist-Catholic Dialogue.

John Fea is Professor of History and Chair of the History Department at Messiah College in Mechanicsburg, PA. He is the author or editor of five books, including *Was America Founded as a Christian Nation?: A Historical Introduction.*

Daniel Finn teaches economics and Christian ethics at St. John's University and the College of St. Benedict and is the director of the True Wealth of Nations research project at the Institute for Advanced Catholic Studies at the University of Southern California. He holds a doctorate from the University of Chicago, and his books include *Christian Economic Ethics: History and Implications, The Moral Ecology of Markets: A Framework for Assessing Justice in Economic Life,* and *Empirical Foundations of the Common Good: What Theology Can Learn from Social Science.*

David P. Gushee is Distinguished University Professor of Christian Ethics and Director of the Center for Theology and Public Life at Mercer University. The author or editor of twenty-two books, he is currently the president of the American Academy of Religion.

Stephen V. Monsma was professor of Political Science at Calvin College and Pepperdine University; a member of the house and senate of the Michigan State legislature; and author of many books.

Leo J. O'Donovan, SJ, is president emeritus of Georgetown University and currently Director of Mission for Jesuit Refugee Service/USA. He holds a doctorate in theology from the University of Muenster, where he studied under Karl Rahner, SJ, and has also been for many years now an art critic publishing in American and European journals.

Cheryl J. Sanders is Senior Pastor of the Third Street Church of God in Washington, DC and Professor of Christian Ethics at the Howard University School of Divinity. She is the author of *Ministry at the Margins*; *Saints in Exile*; *Empowerment Ethics for a Liberated People;* and an edited volume, *Living the Intersection*. She is a graduate of Swarthmore College and Harvard Divinity School.

Ronald J. Sider is Distinguished Professor of Theology, Holistic Ministry, and Public Policy at Palmer Seminary at Eastern University; founder and President emeritus of Evangelicals for Social Action; and author of many books, including *Rich Christians in an Age of Hunger.*

Glen Harold Stassen was Lewis B. Smedes Professor of Christian Ethics at Fuller Theological Seminary from 1996 until his death in 2014. He was the author of *Just Peacemaking* and *A Thicker Jesus*, among other notable works.

Introduction

POPE FRANCIS'S CLOSE FRIENDSHIP with prominent evangelical evangelist Luis Palau is a visible personal symbol of a much broader Catholic-evangelical dialogue that this book represents. The personal friendship between Pope Francis and Luis Palau is but one aspect of a refreshing change in attitude that the pope witnesses on a global stage but which has been developing in numerous local relationships.

Pope Francis is the first Bishop of Rome to visit the Waldensian Evangelical Church, the centuries-old evangelical Protestant church in Italy. He did this partly because he already had experienced "meetings with friends of the Waldensian Evangelical Church of the River Plate" in his native Argentina and partly because his vision of ecumenism calls for us to join together "to continue to journey together" and "together to meet today's men and women, who at times seem so distracted and indifferent, to pass on to them the heart of the Gospel."[1] That was in 2015 at the Waldensian Temple in Turin. Pope Francis apologized to Waldensians "for unchristian-like and even inhuman attitudes and conduct which, historically, we have had against you" and then invited cooperation and joint efforts for the sake of the gospel.

A year earlier, in 2014, Pope Francis visited the Pentecostal Church of Reconciliation in Caserta, south of Rome, in the Campania region of Italy. The visit was at the request of its pastor, Giovanni Traettino. News of the forthcoming visit was both a surprise and a source of shock, particularly to the Catholics of Caserta. So the pope kindly visited the Catholic diocese of Caserta two days in advance, held an open forum with the clergy, and prayed

1. Pastoral Visit of His Holiness Pope Francis to Turin, Visit to the Waldensian Temple, Address of the Holy Father, June 22, 2015, http://w2.vatican.va/content/francesco/en/speeches/2015/june/documents/papa-francesco_20150622_torino-chiesa-valdese.html.

with the people of the diocese. To the Catholic clergy, he reiterated that "We must not be a Church closed in on herself, which watches her navel, a self-referential Church, who looks at herself and is unable to transcend."[2] Then, two days later, the pope defined his understanding of ecumenism in action, when he met with the Pentecostal Congregation: "It is on this path that we Christians do what we call by the theological name of ecumenism: we seek to ensure that this diversity may be more harmonized by the Holy Spirit and become unity; we try to walk before God and be blameless; we try to go and find the nourishment we need to find our brother."[3] While these two visits in Italy have global significance for Catholics and evangelicals, they are also examples of how much on the world stage of ecumenism depends on solid, locally based relationships. To paraphrase an American politician, all ecumenism is local ecumenism.

Evangelical-Catholic conversation and dialogue have experienced enormous growth in the last fifty years, although we all know that there are numerous, significant theological issues that still divide us.[4] Thank God that most Catholics and most Evangelicals no longer say horrible things about each other. Thank God that they increasingly recognize each other as sisters and brothers in Christ. Thank God that unlike 1960 most Protestants no longer oppose a presidential candidate just because s/he is a Catholic—and vice versa. Thank God that evangelicals and Catholics today focus more on the theological commitments we share than the ones that still divide us.[5] What we together confess—that God is Father, Son and Holy Spirit; that Jesus Christ is true God and true man; that Jesus rose bodily from the

2. Visit of the Holy Father to Caserta, Meeting with the Clergy, July 26, 2014, http://w2.vatican.va/content/francesco/en/speeches/2014/july/documents/papa-frances-co_20140726_clero-caserta.html.

3. Private Visit of the Holy Father to Caserta, July 28, 2014, http://w2.vatican.va/content/francesco/en/speeches/2014/july/documents/papa-francesco_20140728_caserta-pastore-traettino.html.

4. For an overview of the history, see William M. Shea, *The Lion and the Lamb: Evangelicals and Catholics in America* (New York: Oxford University Press, 2004). For an example of dialogue, see Basil Meeking and John Stott, eds. *The Evangelical-Roman Catholic Dialogue on Mission: 1977–1984* (Exeter: Paternoster, 1986).

5. Evangelical historian Mark A. Noll coauthored (with Carolyn Nystrom) a book called *Is the Reformation Over? An Evangelical Assessment of Contemporary Roman Catholicism* (Grand Rapids: Baker Academic, 2005). See also the book by evangelical scholars, *The Legacy of John Paul II: An Evangelical Assessment*, ed. Tim Perry (Downers Grove, IL: IVP Academic, 2007); and the essays in Thomas P. Rausch, ed., *Catholics and Evangelicals: Do They Share a Common Future?* (New York: Paulist, 2000).

dead; that Jesus' life, death, and resurrection, made present through the continuing ministry of the church, are the means of salvation for all; and that the Word of God, written under the inspiration of the Holy Spirit in the Bible, is God's unique, reliable special revelation—is huge and worthy of great celebration.

In the last several decades, Catholics and evangelicals in many places and certainly in the US have become allies in significant public policy debates. First in the case of abortion and the sanctity of life, then in the area of marriage, and more recently in the struggle to combat poverty and care for creation, evangelicals and Catholics have found common ground and joined together in numerous public policy debates.[6]

The specific process that prompted the essays in this book began when evangelical and Catholic scholars compared official Catholic and evangelical documents on social policy. When the board of the National Association of Evangelicals (the largest evangelical body in the United States, representing 30 million Evangelicals) unanimously endorsed *For the Health of the Nation* in 2004 as its official framework for public policy engagement,[7] scholars quickly pointed out that there was enormous overlap with the official Catholic teaching on social policy. In response, John Borelli at (Catholic) Georgetown University and Ronald J. Sider at (evangelical) Eastern University organized a series of three-day annual conferences to probe the extent of this common ground. The group took two documents—the Pontifical Council for Justice and Peace's *Compendium of the Social Doctrine of the Church* and the NAE's *For the Health of the Nation*—as their foundational texts for the ongoing exploration. The several-year dialogue discovered differences as well as agreement, but certainly confirmed the early intuition that there is enormous convergence in the thinking on social policy in Catholic and evangelical circles.

The essays in this book probe both the differences and the common ground. And also reflect on the potential significance of much greater evangelical-Catholic cooperation on the numerous positions they share. Only the future will reveal how that cooperation might develop. But the

6. For the historic 1994 document "Evangelicals and Catholics Together," see Charles Colson and Richard John Neuhaus, eds., *Evangelicals and Catholics Together: Toward a Common Mission* (Dallas: Word, 1995). In the section on public engagement, this document reflects (by what it says and what it omits) a more conservative political agenda.

7. Ronald J. Sider and Diane Knippers, eds., *Toward an Evangelical Public Policy: Political Strategies for the Health of the Nation* (Grand Rapids: Baker, 2005), 363–75; see also 9–11.

enormously positive response that Pope Francis meets as he humbly, warmly models broad ecumenical dialogue and calls powerfully for economic justice and creation care as we continue to affirm the sanctity of human life and marriage generates hope that substantial Catholic-evangelical dialogue and cooperation has only just begun. The authors of these essays hope and pray that it will grow and mature in the next few decades.

As this book was in the final steps of preparation, the publication of an article by a Catholic and Protestant, Antonio Spadaro, SJ, editor-in-chief of *La Civiltà Cattolica*, and Marcelo Figueroa, Presbyterian pastor, editor-in-chief of the Argentinian edition of *L'Osservatore Romano*, caused quite a stir in Catholic and evangelical circles for its criticism of a troublesome alliance of some Catholics and Protestants evident on the political scene of the United States. They criticized "a Manichaean language that divides reality between absolute Good and absolute Evil" that drives wedges and divisions within society, separating from "the community of believers" those who are perceived as threats to Christian culture and life. The essays in this book represent a different attitude from those who preach hate, who shun inclusion, and who emphasize the gospel of prosperity. Evangelicals and Catholics working together for the common good would agree with a May 9, 2017, statement of Pope Francis cited by the authors of that essay that "The contribution of Christianity to a culture is that of Christ washing feet, or the service and the gift of life."[8]

John Borelli
Ronald J. Sider

---

8. "Evangelical Fundamentalism and Catholic Integralism in the USA: A surprising ecumenism,"*La Civiltà Cattolica*, July 13, 2017, http://www.laciviltacattolica.it/articolo/evangelical-fundamentalism-and-catholic-integralism-in-the-usa-a-surprising-ecumenism/.

PART ONE

From Hostility to Cooperation

1

A Brief History of Modern Evangelical Social Engagement in America

JOHN FEA

IN 1873, EVANGELICAL CHRISTIANS met in New York City for the Sixth General Conference of the Evangelical Alliance. The Evangelical Alliance was an international organization with a nondenominational focus. Anyone was invited to participate who could affirm a belief in the inspiration of the Bible, the Trinity, the depravity of human nature, the incarnation of Jesus Christ and his atonement for sins, justification by faith alone, the work of the Holy Spirit in the world, and the resurrection of the body. Since this was a gathering that met only every few years, it was the equivalent of an evangelical Olympic Games. The minutes of the conference and the addresses delivered by the participants provide a revealing snapshot of American evangelicalism in the wake of the Civil War.

In addition to the usual evangelical presentations on the need to evangelize the world and the "threat" of "Romanism," sessions at the meeting of the Evangelical Alliance were also devoted to the labor problem, the importance of upholding the separation of church and state, religious liberty, temperance, Sabbath reform, the family, Christian unity, world religions, the dangers of wealth and materialism, the role of education in society, the care of the sick, the industrial revolution, and crime. Few topics escaped coverage during this eleven-day meeting. There was even a session on cruelty to animals.

William G. Allen, the president of Girard College in Philadelphia, gave a talk on the labor problem in the United States. He called upon labor interests to stop their violent strikes and use their power to "promote peace on earth and good will among men." The resources devoted to waging "war" against big business might be better used to "feed the hungry and clothe the naked." Was it too much to ask "nationals professing Christ," Girard asked, to be "imbued with something of the spirit of Christ?"

Labor, of course, was only part of the problem. Allen urged the US government to support the eight-hour workday, require that labor disputes be decided through arbitration rather than violent strikes, design equitable apprenticeship laws, reserve public lands for settlers rather than railroad companies and speculators, and establish a bureau of labor statistics. While Allen believed that evangelicals could support many of the reforms advocated by the labor movement, he rejected the movement's attempts at preventing immigration from China. If unions were willing to promote "the solidarity of labor and co-operation of working men everywhere" they should not make distinctions between European and Asian workers. His address both supported capitalism and defended labor. The goal was reconciliation, a virtue fitting of a "nation professing Christ." [1]

Labor reform and Sabbath reform went hand in hand at the meeting of the Evangelical Alliance. An address by Reverend Mark Hopkins, the former president of Williams College, urged the federal government to pass laws protecting the observance of the Christian Sabbath. Hopkins argued that the Fourth Commandment should be embedded in American law much in the same way that commandments prohibiting murder, stealing, and "bearing false witness" were staples of the legal system. If that was not enough for the naysayers, Hopkins emphasized Jesus' words in Mark 2:27: "The Sabbath was made for man, not man for the Sabbath." He argued that the human body was created by God in such a way that it required a day of rest. "Men and animals," Hopkins argued, will have better health and live longer, will do more work, and do it better if they rest one day in seven, than if they work continuously. Rest was a human right endowed by God. If this were true, then how could a nation with Christian roots not endorse the Sabbath? [2]

1. William H. Allen, "The Labor Question," in *History, Essays, Orations, and Other Documents of the Sixth General Conference of the Evangelical Alliance.*, ed. Philip Schaff and Irenaeus Prime (New York: Harper and Brothers, 1874), 670–74.

2. Reverend Mark Hopkins, "The Sabbath Made for Men—His Consequent Right to Legislation for Serving Its Ends," in ibid., 540–44.

Like the movement to preserve the Christian Sabbath, temperance reform had long been part of the social consciousness of American evangelicals. Though the opposition to slavery had been the most prominent Northern evangelical reform effort in the early nineteenth century, it was now time, with the Civil War over and the Thirteenth Amendment passed, to focus the nation again on temperance. This was the sentiment of Lane Theological Seminary professor Henry A. Nelson in his address "Intemperance and Its Suppression." Nelson's arguments were typical of evangelical crusades against alcohol. The "drunkard" was a "sinner against God" and a "criminal also toward civil society." He disrespected his body, debased his intellect, desolated his home and family, loaded society with the "burdens of taxation," and contributed to national vices that led to the "hopeless ruin of souls by rendering them incapable of receiving the Gospel." Much of Nelson's argument countered those libertarian-minded Americans who believed that government enforcement of morality in this area was a violation of their civil rights. While Nelson admitted that this was indeed a thorny issue, he concluded that the practice of giving Americans the right to drink excessively would ultimately violate the rights of others.[3]

All of these addresses were typical of the speeches on social reform at the 1873 meeting of the Evangelical Alliance. Not only did the speakers at the conference address the social problems of the day from a biblical perspective, but they also discussed the social and economic structures that led to these ills. This large conference was one of the last great flourishes of a nineteenth-century American culture dominated by evangelicalism and evangelical social concern. Evangelicals led the way on most important moral issues of the day—slavery, temperance, women's rights, prison reform, and the alleviation of poverty. According to one speaker at the conference, it was the task of evangelical churches to "educate the State in the Christian ethics of government," whether the issue was labor-capital relations, the preservation of the Sabbath, or the crusade against intemperance.[4]

I raise the history of the Evangelical Alliance here not to necessarily endorse or reject any of the specific social issues that concerned evangelicals in 1873, but to show that late nineteenth-century evangelicals were indeed engaged with moral and social issues that they believed were important for preserving a healthy, if not a "Christian" nation.[5]

---

3. Reverend Henry A. Nelson, "Intemperance and Its Suppression," in ibid., 689–94.

4. Ibid.

5. Much of this section draws from John Fea, *Was America Founded as a Christian*

At the turn of the twentieth century, evangelicalism—if you could even use that name to describe a diverse group of conservative Protestants—was a big tent. It included urban evangelists like Dwight L. Moody, who promoted no real social agenda apart from winning new converts to Christ. In Moody's words, "I look on this world as a wrecked vessel. God has given me a lifeline and said to me 'Moody save all you can.'" It included reform-minded populist politicians like William Jennings Bryan, who railed against corporate capitalism and fought against the economic structures of society that were oppressing common men and women. It included the Salvation Army, the YMCA, and others committed to bringing "salvation to the slums." It included Billy Sunday, who succeeded Moody as America's next great evangelist and teamed with progressives in the fight against what he called "demon rum." And it included black evangelicals who could be found in churches such as The Church of God in Christ, a new and influential expression of the Holiness Movement that would eventually blossom into a vibrant form of black Pentecostalism.[6]

Yet by the 1920s a gathering like that which occurred at the Evangelical Alliance meeting in New York would have been inconceivable. What happened?

Evangelicals had a strong reaction against liberal Protestants who would come to embrace the social gospel movement. Around the turn of the twentieth century a group of Protestants put forward a new brand of Christianity concerned more with improving *this* world than preparing one's soul for the next world. The leaders of the social gospel movement believed that by meeting social needs the United States could build a Christian civilization that would herald the second coming of Jesus Christ. Social gospelers set out to Christianize America through reforms, government programs, and voluntary societies designed to tackle the social problems—poverty, disease, and immorality—resulting from industrialization, urbanization, and immigration. The difference between the social gospelers

Nation?: A Historical Introduction (Louisville: Westminster John Knox, 2011), 25–29.

6. Dwight Lyman Moody and W. H. Daniels, *Moody: His Words, His Work, and Workers* (Chicago: Walden, 1877), 476; Michael Kazin, *A Godly Hero: The Life of William Jennings Bryan* (New York: Knopf, 2006); John Fea, "The Town That Billy Sunday Could Not Shut Down: Prohibition and Sunday's Chicago Crusade of 1918," *Illinois Historical Journal* 87 (1994), 250; Anne H. Pinn and Anthony B. Pinn, *Fortress Introduction to Black Church History* (Minneapolis: Fortress, 2002), 102–24. For a discussion of turn of the twentieth-century evangelicalism see George M. Marsden, *Fundamentalism and American Culture: The Shaping of Twentieth-Century Evangelicalism, 1870–1925* (New York: Oxford University Press, 1980).

and the evangelicals of the nineteenth century was largely related to differences in theology.[7]

Protestant liberals were often described as "modernists" because of their willingness to conform their theological convictions to modern culture. Many believed in the authority of the Bible for matters of faith and practice, but understood it more as a *witness to God* than the *word of God*. Some liberals believed in a creator-God, but thought that this God worked through the science of evolution. They tended to reject the doctrine of original sin, the existence of Satan and hell, the need for a conversion experience, and the virgin birth of Jesus Christ. Ultimately, they tied their theological wagons to the train of progress. Society was advancing toward the kingdom of God and Christians needed to play a part in its coming.[8]

Meanwhile, evangelicals, who were now beginning to rally around a multi-volume 1910 publication called "The Fundamentals," disagreed with liberal Protestants on every major theological issue. J. Gresham Machen, a professor at the conservative Princeton Theological Seminary, did not even think modernists were Christians. Many evangelicals (but not all of them) were embracing an eschatological vision—known as premillennialism—which taught the imminent return of Jesus Christ. Premillennialism called evangelicals to convert people to Christianity, thus securing their place in heaven, and then wait expectantly for the return of Jesus. In other words, they were not responsible, like the postmillennial theology that social gospelers and liberal Protestants had taught, to usher in the kingdom of God through social reform. Some of these premillennialists, such as C. I. Scofield, the author of the wildly popular Scofield Reference Bible, believed that the teachings of Jesus in the Gospels were not even directly applicable to modern Christians.[9] Granted, evangelicals continued with their inner city rescue missions and work with the urban poor, but they seldom explored the deeper social, economic, historical, jurisprudential, and political reasons behind such social injustice. The goal was to get people saved.[10]

7. Susan Curtis, *A Consuming Faith: The Social Gospel and Modern American Culture* (Baltimore: The Johns Hopkins University Press, 1991), 2, 3; Robert T. Handy, *A Christian America: Protestant Hopes and Historical Realities*, 2nd ed. (New York: Oxford University Press, 1984), 140, 144.

8. William R. Hutchison, *The Modernist Impulse in American Protestantism* (Cambridge, MA: Harvard University Press, 1976), 2.

9. Marsden, *Fundamentalism and American Culture.*

10. On premillennialism and fundamentalism, see Matthew Sutton, *American Apocalypse: A History of American Evangelicalism* (Cambridge, MA: Harvard University Press, 2014).

According to historian George Marsden, World War I was the decisive moment that turned evangelicals into fundamentalists. Many evangelicals were cautious about throwing their support behind America's entrance into the war. William Jennings Bryan, an evangelical and the Secretary of State in Woodrow Wilson's administration, resigned his position because he opposed US involvement. But as it turned out, Bryan was an exception to the rule. Most evangelicals, despite initial hesitations, decided to support the war. Billy Sunday, for example, wrote in 1917 that "Christianity and Patriotism are synonymous terms and hell and traitors are synonymous." Other evangelicals linked German higher criticism—the belief that the Bible was not God-inspired and should be read and interpreted much like any other piece of literature—with the German war machine. Fundamentalists viewed World War I as a battle against both the Kaiser and the German university. Even premillennialists were able to rid themselves of their otherworldliness for a time in order to support the American cause overseas. Following the war, American evangelicals transferred their opposition to Germany into a fight for control of their denominations. In 1920 Baptist editor Curtis Lee Laws coined the term "fundamentalist" to describe an evangelical who was willing to "do battle royal for the Fundamentals [of the Christian faith]." Evangelicals feared a liberal takeover of their denominations by Protestants who denied traditional Christian doctrines such as the inerrancy of the Bible and the virgin birth. They believed that these theological liberals undermined the Christian civilization they hoped to sustain.[11]

Opposition to Darwinian evolution—the belief that human beings came into existence through the process of natural selection and the "survival of the fittest"—was a major rallying point for fundamentalists. The battle again Darwinism was important for fundamentalists because it affected the education of their children. If the next generation of Americans believed that humans descended from monkeys, what would happen to Christian civilization in the United States? Fundamentalists put a lot of energy into winning the fight against evolution. In 1925, when William Jennings Bryan heard that John Scopes, a schoolteacher in Dayton, Tennessee, had violated state law by teaching evolution to his science classes, he enlisted in the battle. The American Civil Liberties Union chose Dayton as a test case in their crusade to banish laws forbidding the teaching of evolution in schools and hired famed trial lawyer Clarence Darrow to defend Scopes. Bryan volunteered his services to the prosecution. In the end,

11. Marsden, *Fundamentalism and American Culture*, 149–53.

Bryan would win the case against Scopes, but the trial was an utter disaster for the fundamentalist movement. Darrow called Bryan to the stand as an expert witness and proceeded to embarrass him before a room of national print and radio reporters. Bryan was not a theologian or a scientist. He thus sounded foolish trying to answer Darrow's questions. Bryan passed away five days after the trial ended, and the fundamentalist movement went with him. These militant evangelicals lost control of their denominations and their hold on American culture. Their mission of creating a Christian civilization had failed.[12]

After the intellectual and cultural embarrassment of the Scopes Trial in 1925 evangelicals left the public square and turned inward, forming their own subculture of radio stations, Bible colleges, parachurch organizations, foreign mission societies, and publishing houses. During the 1930s these organizations had very little contact with mainstream American culture and were certainly not participating in anything close to what today we might call "public engagement." As historian Joel Carpenter has shown, this turn away from the larger culture did not mean that evangelicals were abandoning their desire to influence America for Christ. They continued to dream of a Christian nation and used these new parachurch organizations to leaven the culture. Eventually the major players in the subculture, people like Billy Graham, theologian Carl F. H. Henry, and Boston pastor John Harold Ockenga, would emerge from their enclaves in the 1940s to form the National Association of Evangelicals (NAE). But even then, the NAE had little influence in shaping the culture. If they were speaking with a prophetic voice, no one was really listening.[13]

But that does not mean that they did not make efforts. Evangelicals continued to think about "the health of the nation" in their own way. If they were no longer the custodians of the culture, they could still forge a Christian America by winning people to Christ. A nation of born-again Christians who practiced their faith in everyday life would lead to the restoration of an evangelical culture in the United States. Evangelicals relied upon the power of the Holy Spirit to awaken the churches amid this season of cultural impotence.

At the first meeting of the NAE, Harold John Ockenga, the organization's first president, delivered an addressed entitled "Christ for America."

12. Ibid., 184–88.

13. Joel Carpenter, *Revive Us Again: The Reawakening of American Fundamentalism* (New York: Oxford University Press, 1997); Molly Worthen, *Apostles of Reason: The Crisis of Authority in American Evangelicalism* (New York: Oxford University Press, 2013).

He called upon the long-standing American belief, dating back to the seventeenth-century Puritans, that the United States had a mission on the earth akin to that of Old Testament Israel. America, Ockenga believed, was on the verge of a great religious revival. He urged the members of the NAE to "become the vanguard for the reconstruction of society's foundations." The NAE also became strong supporters of a "Christian Amendment" to the US Constitution. In 1947 and 1954 the organization promoted an effort to add the following words to the Constitution: "This nation divinely recognizes the authority and law of Jesus Christ, Savior and Ruler of Nations through whom are bestowed the blessings of Almighty God."[14]

Of course evangelicals also wed their hopes for the preservation of a healthy nation to revival meetings conducted by charismatic preachers. No one was better suited to fulfill this role than Billy Graham. While Graham always understood his ministry to be more about winning souls than forging a cultural agenda for the nation, he probably did more to contribute to the cultural and social vision of evangelicals than any other figure. The young Graham railed against American's moral problems. His messages were filled with jeremiads against divorce, promiscuous sex, materialism, alcohol abuse, and crime. The only way to overcome these social problems eroding the moral fabric of the United States was for individuals to turn to Jesus Christ. The Cold War often served as a backdrop for Graham's sermons, many of which included anticommunist rants.[15]

The evangelical social vision in the 1930s, 1940s, 1950s, and much of the 1960s was to promote a Christian nation through evangelistic preaching and revivalism, fight atheistic communism, rest comfortably as a contributor to Eisenhower's civil religion, and eventually become part of Nixon's silent majority. When in 1947 Carl F. H. Henry challenged evangelicals to think about their social responsibilities in his book *The Uneasy Conscience of Modern Fundamentalism*, fellow evangelicals viewed him as a radical. Henry's call for Christians to care about things like aggressive warfare, racial hatred and intolerance, the liquor traffic, and the exploitation of labor largely fell on deaf ears.[16] Even Henry himself eventually backed off.

14. Carpenter, *Revive Us Again*, 149; Isaac Kramnick and Laurence Moore, *The Godless Constitution: The Case Against Religious Correctness* (New York: W. W. Norton, 1997), 148.

15. William Martin, *A Prophet with Honor: The Billy Graham Story* (New York: William Morrow, 1991), 91, 101, 115–16; Carpenter, *Revive Us Again*, 221–22.

16. Henry, *The Uneasy Conscience of Modern Fundamentalism* (Grand Rapids: Eerdmans, 1947).

Twenty-five or thirty years later, in the pages of *Christianity Today*, a publication that he edited, Henry returned to a time-worn twentieth century evangelical theme by arguing strongly that the best way for evangelicals to respond to the civil rights movement and the Vietnam War was to pray for a spiritual revival.

But not all evangelicals remained quiet during the tumult of the 1960s. African American evangelicals were at the forefront of the civil rights movement. Theologians and activists such as John Perkins, Tom Skinner, and Bill Pannell formed organizations that fought for black civil rights and sought to meet the spiritual and physical needs of poor blacks in the South. Many of these black evangelicals came out of the black holiness and Pentecostal churches that grew up around the turn of the twentieth century. They used their growing popularity to challenge evangelicals to fight racial prejudice and the injustices of the American economic and political system. In the process, they criticized white evangelicals, especially those who continued to uphold a theology that taught that the black race, as descendants of Noah's son Ham, were cursed and relegated to lives of servitude.[17] In 1963, a group of black evangelicals with roots in the Churches of God in Christ, white fundamentalist movements of the 1920s, and Holiness movements such as the Christian Missionary Alliance, formed the National Negro Evangelical Association (the name was eventually changed to the National Black Evangelical Association [NBEA]). Though the primary purpose of the NBEA was to spread the gospel and win souls for Christ, the leadership of the organization could not help but get involved in the social issues of the day. Debate raged within the organization over whether the primary focus of the NBEA should be to preach the gospel or to spread the "good news" alongside an active mission to promote social justice. Many black evangelicals began to embrace the social justice agenda of the Black Theology movement (while rejecting the movement's failure to uphold a high view of the authority of the Bible) in an attempt to situate the NBEA in the historic African American church, particularly in terms of activism. By the 1990s, the NBEA was discussing the viability of dropping the term "evangelical" because of its connection to white political conservatism.[18]

17. David Swartz, "Left Behind: The Evangelical Left and the Limits of Evangelical Politics, 1965–1988," (PhD diss., University of Notre Dame, 2008), 167–78.

18. Albert G. Miller, "National Black Evangelical Association," in *Encyclopedia of African American Culture and History*, eds. Jack Salzman, David Lionel Smith, and Cornell West (New York: Macmillan, 1996), 1955–57; Albert G. Miller, "The Rise of African-American Evangelicalism in American Culture," in *Perspectives on American Religion and Culture*, ed. Peter Williams (Oxford: Blackwell, 1999), 259–69.

In the late 1960s and into the early 1970s, a growing number of "young evangelicals," as they were called at the time, were not satisfied with this evangelical approach to social issues. Many of them were white, suburban, middle-class Americans who began to notice that the evangelicalism in which they were raised did not mesh very well with a 1960s youth culture that challenged capitalism, protested Vietnam, mocked the middle class, and fought for human and civil rights. Socially conscious groups of students emerged at evangelical colleges such as Wheaton, Houghton, Messiah, Calvin, Gordon, Seattle Pacific, and Westmont. Jim Wallis, an activist working with Students for a Democratic Society at Michigan State University, founded the Post-American community (later Sojourners) at Trinity Evangelical Divinity School in the Chicago suburb of Deerfield. Some of these young evangelicals were taken by the works of John Howard Yoder, a Mennonite theologian who challenged Constantinianism, taught a radical form of Christian pacifism, and pushed for a vision of public engagement that centered on the church as a political community called to speak truth to power. Others took a more Reformed approach to public engagement. These young Calvinists, most of whom were centered around Calvin College in Grand Rapids and the Institute for Christian Studies in Toronto, set out to redeem God's fallen creation and in the process bring a Christian view of justice to every corner of North American life.

Others turned to the writings of the post-fundamentalist apologist Francis Schaeffer (whose book *Pollution and the Death of Man* was chosen as the book of the year by the Environmental Protection Agency in 1970), his student Os Guiness, the author of a massive tome, *The Dust of Death*, that critiqued both the 1960s culture and the evangelical establishment, or progressive theologians such as Clark Pinnock. This group also caught the attention of Mark Hatfield, a liberal Republican senator from Oregon and an evangelical who would serve as an unofficial mentor and benefactor for the movement. A small but vibrant evangelical movement was forming that rejected the godlessness of the New Left and challenged the so-called "silent majority" to end their silence and start living out the social implications of their faith.[19]

In 1972, evangelical historian and activist Ronald Sider spearheaded Evangelicals for McGovern, the first explicitly evangelical organization in

---

19. Much of the section above draws heavily from David R. Swartz, *Moral Minority: The Evangelical Left in an Age of Conservatism* (Philadelphia: University of Pennsylvania Press, 2012).

American history to support a presidential candidate. Roughly one year later a group of young evangelicals who were speaking against the war and in favor of school busing, the ERA, and environmental protection converged at the YMCA in downtown Chicago in an attempt to find some common ground. The meeting produced a statement, known as the Chicago Declaration, which defended the social and economic rights of the poor, oppressed, and marginalized, and attacked the "pathology of war," sexism, and American materialism. Yet, as historian David Swartz argues, the evangelical left was constantly plagued by identity politics. Anabaptist and Reformed members argued over the best Christian and theological approach to promoting social justice. Those attending the 1973 meeting in Chicago and subsequent meetings were divided by questions of race and gender to the point that a quota system needed to be established for choosing delegates to the meetings. The cause of evangelical social justice would go on, but in a very decentralized and splintered fashion.[20]

Evangelical progressives, of course, were not the only ones finding their way back to the public sphere in the 1970s. Many evangelicals believed that the counterculture of the 1960s was challenging the kind of morality necessary for a Christian republic to survive. The feminist movement empowered women in a way that led them to reject what some evangelicals saw as women's God-given place in society. Rock and roll music and the culture that came with it glorified drugs, alcohol, and free sex. In 1962 the Supreme Court, in *Engel v. Vitale,* made prayer in school unconstitutional. A year later, in *Abington Township School District v. Schempp,* the high court ended Bible reading in public schools. Though a "silent majority" of conservatives would manage to vote Richard Nixon into office in 1968, the culture had apparently given way to forces intent upon undermining the idea of a Christian America.

In the early 1970s two significant Supreme Court cases galvanized evangelicals who were concerned about the health of the nation. In *Green v. Connally* (1971) the Supreme Court ruled that a private school or college that discriminated on the basis of race would no longer be considered for tax-exempt status. At the heart of this controversy was Bob Jones University, a school that banned interracial dating and denied admission to unmarried African Americans. In 1975 the IRS moved to revoke the tax-exempt status of the university. *Green v. Connally* would also have implications for the hundreds of private Christian schools cropping up all

20. This section rests heavily on ibid.

over the United States. Many of these schools were in the South and had discriminatory admissions policies. When Jimmy Carter, a self-proclaimed born-again Christian, threw his support behind the *Green v. Connally* decision, he alienated many evangelicals who had supported him in 1976, including Jerry Falwell, Christian psychologist James Dobson, and activist Paul Weyrich. These conservatives believed that the president and the Supreme Court were undermining the liberty of Christians to form their own schools in their own way, without interference from the federal government. By 1976, the year that *Newsweek* proclaimed "The Year of the Evangelical," the so-called Christian Right had organized into a full-blown political movement.[21]

The second major Supreme Court case that mobilized the Christian Right was *Roe v. Wade*, which legalized certain types of abortion in the United States. Prior to *Roe v. Wade* abortion had never been an important issue for evangelicals. Most evangelicals believed abortion was morally suspect, but thought of opposition to abortion as a distinctly Catholic cause. This all changed, however, after 1973. More and more evangelicals began to publicly oppose abortion and *Roe v. Wade*. Many of them were awakened to a belief that abortion was equivalent to legalized murder.

The leaders of this new Christian Right found theological and philosophical support for their views from the teachings of Francis Schaeffer. From his chalet in the Swiss Alps called L'Abri, Schaeffer had developed a reputation as a thoughtful evangelical at a time when the movement lacked serious intellectual depth. He attracted hundreds of bright young evangelical minds to L'Abri, where he taught them how to formulate a "Christian worldview." By the mid-1970s Schaeffer was a household name among American evangelicals. Following *Roe v. Wade* he also became convinced that the fight against abortion was worth his time and energy. In a popular film series entitled *How Should We Then Live*, Schaeffer challenged *Roe v. Wade* on legal and philosophical grounds and defended the dignity of all human life. His ideas were soon being used by Falwell and other members of the Christian Right.[22]

So where does this leave us? Since 1980, the Christian Right has defined for the general public what it means to be a civically responsible

---

21. I am following the argument here of Randall Balmer, *Thy Kingdom Come: An Evangelical's Lament* (New York: Basic, 2006), 13–17.

22. Barry Hankins, *Francis Schaeffer and the Shaping of Evangelical America* (Grand Rapids: Eerdmans, 2008), 175–77, 180–91, 198–202.

evangelical. Its leaders continue to understand Christian activism in terms of two or three social issues. And as long as conservative evangelicals remain concerned with abortion and gay marriage, the Christian Right will continue to have traction in American life and in the Republican Party. This was seen clearly in the recent 2016 election as evangelicals flocked in large numbers to the candidacy of Donald Trump largely because the New York businessman promised to promote conservative Supreme Court justices who would rule favorably on the moral issues important to them. In other words, I don't think the Christian Right is going away any time soon, but I am a historian, and these kinds of predictions take me beyond my pay grade.

Meanwhile, the evangelical middle and left toiled in relative obscurity during the 1980s and 1990s until the Democrats found God in the wake of the 2004 presidential elections and called upon Jim Wallis and other progressive Christians for help. The willingness of Democrats to entertain the possibility of thinking theologically about their political agenda opened the door for a more nuanced and comprehensive conversation about evangelical social action. As Christian Right founders pass from the scene, a new group of evangelical leaders such as Bill Hybels, Rick Warren, and Joel Hunter have challenged evangelicals to rethink their commitment to social justice and embrace a consistent and comprehensive ethic of life.

Evangelical young people, many of them connected with "emerging churches" that meet in coffeehouses and shopping malls, are getting their politics and understanding of cultural engagement from evangelical progressives such as Shane Claiborne and Brian McClaren.[23] Columnists like Nicholas Kristof consistently praise evangelicals working to alleviate poverty in Darfur and stopping sex trafficking around the globe.[24] Compassionate Christian conservatives are engaged in fighting HIV/AIDS; and evangelicals continue to defend the right of the unborn and institutions of marriage and family. James Davison Hunter, in his recent book *To Change the World*, has challenged evangelicals—of the left, right, and neo-Anabaptist persuasions to stop trying to change the world through

---

23. Shane Claiborne, *The Irresistible Revolution: Living as an Ordinary Radical* (Grand Rapids: Zondervan, 2006); Brian McLaren, *A New Kind of Christian: A Tale of Two Friends on a Spiritual Journey* (Jossey-Bass, 2001).

24. See, for example, Nicholas Kristof, "Evangelicals a Liberal Can Love," *New York Times*, February 3, 2008.

politics and instead consider social change through faithful presence in their communities.[25]

Marcia Pally, a scholar at New York University, has recently argued that today's younger evangelicals are dissatisfied with the model of political engagement associated with the Christian Right. If Pally is correct, it looks as if the next generation of evangelicals will be staunch defenders of religious liberty and the separation of church and state. They will champion economic justice, fight for environmental protection under the umbrella of "creation care," and continue to engage in humanitarian aid abroad. Younger evangelicals oppose gay marriage, but they also oppose anti-gay discrimination in housing, education, and non-religious employments. Pally notes that they may believe homosexuality is a sin, but also believe that democracies "do not punish people for their sins." They oppose abortion, but do not believe that this is the only moral ill that Christians must confront.[26]

It appears that the National Association of Evangelicals is moving with these young evangelicals. In 2004, The Evangelical Project for Public Engagement produced a document titled *For the Health of the Nation: An Evangelical Call to Civic Responsibility*. It called evangelicals to address seven spheres of social involvement, including religious freedom, family life, the protection of children, sanctity of life, caring for the poor and vulnerable, human rights, peacemaking, and caring for creation. *For the Health of the Nation* was a clear sign that evangelicals, at least those denominations represented by the National Association of Evangelicals, were interested in ridding themselves of the trappings of the Christian Right and embracing a nineteenth-century vision for Christian social engagement. I am sure those in attendance at the 1873 meeting of the Evangelical Alliance would have read this document and been proud.[27]

25. James Davison Hunter, *To Change the World: The Irony, Tragedy, and Possibility of Christianity in the Late Modern World* (New York: Oxford University Press, 2010).

26. Marcia Pally, *The New Evangelicals: Expanding the Vision of the Common Good* (Grand Rapids: Eerdmans, 2011). Also Pally, "Evangelicals Who Have Left the Right," published at Immanent Frame, http://blogs.ssrc.org/tif/2013/01/15/evangelicals-who-have-left-the-right/.

27. *For the Health of the Nation: An Evangelical Call to Civic Responsibility*, http://www.nae.net/government-relations/for-the-health-of-the-nation.

2

Evangelical-Catholic Cooperation in Public Policy

GALEN CAREY

As THE SON OF evangelical missionaries to a predominantly Catholic country, I grew up rather skeptical about the idea that evangelicals and Catholics
could or would cooperate about anything. The local Catholic priest warned
our neighbors to have nothing to do with our religion which, he said, came
straight from the devil. For our part, we felt certain that many if not most
Catholics worshiped idols and would wind up in hell. In 1964, our first
converts faced social isolation and even persecution. Vandals broke into
their home and hacked up their Bible with a machete. That mutilated Bible
now sits on a bookshelf in my office.

That same year, more than 6,000 miles away, bishops meeting at the
Vatican II Council approved *Unitatis Redintegratio*, a reevaluation of the
relationship of the Roman Catholic Church and other Christian communities. It is safe to say that neither my parents nor the local priest in our town
knew much about those distant deliberations.

Thirty-five years later, my wife and I returned to the village in which I
grew up, and paid a visit to the Catholic church. We were warmly received
by the current priest, who spoke positively about the evangelical church
that my parents had begun and its contributions to the community.

It is doubtful if relations between evangelicals and Catholics in the
United States were ever as antagonistic as they were in some other countries; though in 1960 the National Association of Evangelicals (NAE) passed

a statement expressing doubt about the potentially conflicted loyalties of a Roman Catholic president of the United States.

Over the years ecumenical relations between our communities have advanced dramatically. As a long-time staff member of World Relief, the humanitarian arm of the NAE, I worked closely with colleagues at Catholic Charities on advocacy for refugees, immigrants, and Americans living in poverty. Overseas, we collaborated with Catholic Relief Service and Caritas on disaster response, maternal and child health initiatives, economic development and HIV/AIDS programming. As a Chicagoan, I appreciated leaders such as Cardinal Joseph Bernardin who spoke of the "seamless garment" or consistent ethic of life, protecting human life and dignity at all stages and in all spheres of social and economic development.

The list of public policy issues on which the NAE and the United States Conference of Catholic Bishops (USCCB) share similar positions is long. We both favor immigration reform that prioritizes human dignity and family unity; responsible care of God's creation; religious freedom for people of all faiths and none; protecting marriage and strengthening families; criminal justice reform that focuses on rehabilitation; reduction and eventual elimination of the threat posed by nuclear weapons; a safety net for the poor at home and international assistance aimed at helping the world's most vulnerable people; reforming the practice of predatory payday lending; protecting the unborn; and rejecting the use of torture, among many other common positions.

NAE and USCCB staff meet frequently both bilaterally and in coalitions. We are founding or long-time participating members of several networks, including the Circle of Protection, Faith for Just Lending, and the Coalition to Preserve Religious Freedom. We have organized joint meetings with members of Congress and the administration, and joint press conferences where Catholic bishops and evangelical leaders discuss public policy concerns. We have submitted joint comments on pending regulations.

When the Obama administration issued regulations requiring many faith-based organizations to include contraception and abortifacients in their health insurance policies, both the NAE and the USCCB strenuously objected. The USCCB found the forced provision of any artificial contraceptive products and services unacceptable. Most evangelicals do not object in general to the provision or use of contraception, except for specific drugs or devices that may cause abortions. However, the NAE strongly protested the inadequacy of the religious exemptions that left both Catholic and evangelical organizations unprotected and set a dangerous precedent for overriding conscience and religious convictions of both individuals and religious institutions.

Catholics and evangelicals share common convictions about the nature of marriage as a gift from God meant to unite man and woman in a relationship of love that provides and cares for the next generation. The NAE and USCCB have joined, with other religious leaders, in several statements articulating our understanding and our concern for both cultural and legal drift from this historic understanding.

In 2015, the NAE and Georgetown University cosponsored an Evangelical-Catholic Summit on Overcoming Poverty, attended by more than 100 evangelical and Catholic leaders from across the political spectrum. We explored the theological, pastoral, and public policy challenges involved in ending extreme poverty. We discovered that our shared concerns far outweighed any differences. A particular highlight was a one-hour panel featuring President Barack Obama, Harvard sociologist Robert Putnam, and American Enterprise Institute President Arthur Brooks.

In view of the large and diverse constituencies that both the NAE and USCCB represent, it has been remarkable that we have been able to agree on so many issues. Where there have been barriers to cooperation, these have only occasionally arisen from substantive differences. More frequently, the somewhat lengthy approval process followed by the USCCB has meant that timely joint statements or action was unrealistic. For its part, the NAE, with a much smaller staff, has faced bandwidth constraints in being able to engage effectively in the many issues of mutual interest.

As a sign of our close relations, the USCCB in 2011 hosted a meeting of the NAE board of directors. NAE leaders have also addressed meetings of Catholic leaders.

Our shared concerns extend far beyond our national borders. In 2014, NAE President Leith Anderson and Cardinal Theodore McCarrick traveled to the Central African Republic, along with Imam Mohamed Magid, to urge evangelical, Catholic, and Muslim religious leaders to cooperate in ending sectarian strife. In 2017, the NAE President was invited to the Vatican to discuss the impact of climate change and what can be done to mitigate it and adapt to its effects.

3

Reflections on Catholics and Evangelicals in Public Life: History and Mission, Assets and Lessons, Directions and Dangers

John Carr

INTRODUCTION

On September 24, 2015, I was honored to be in the US Capitol for Pope Francis's historic address to Congress.[1] My eyes and ears focused mostly on the solitary figure in white delivering a powerful message of respect and challenge for our nation. I also closely watched Vice President Joseph Biden and Speaker John Boehner seated behind Pope Francis. These two Catholic public officials were old enough to remember another historic moment in 1960 when prominent Protestant and evangelical leaders, including Dr. Noman Vincent Peale and Rev. Billy Graham, asserted that a Catholic should not be elected President of the United States because he would take advice and guidance from the pope.[2] Fifty-five years later, a Catholic Vice

---

1. "Transcript: Pope Francis's Speech to Congress," *Washington Post*, September 24, 2015.

2. "Religious Issue Plays Major Role in Campaign," *CQ Almanac 1960*, 16th ed., *Congressional Quarterly*, 1960, 11-804–11-808. See also Mark S. Massa, SJ, *Anti-Catholicism in America: The Last Acceptable Prejudice* (New York: Crossroad, 2003), 91–92.

President and a Catholic Speaker were on the rostrum representing different parties and legislative bodies at a time when one of the few things Members of Congress could agree on was that they needed advice and guidance from this pope.

Also in 1960, the National Association of Evangelicals (NAE) produced a pamphlet for "Christian Conviction Sunday" before the election that read:

> Dear Pastor, if a Roman Catholic is elected President, then what? The Church of Rome will have a new, great advantage and the United States will no longer be recognized as a Protestant nation in the eyes of the world. Don't you agree that it is time for the Protestants of the country to stand up and be counted?[3]

It is important to recognize that evangelical Protestants were not the only Americans voicing religious prejudice. It would be several more years before the Second Vatican Council defended the religious freedom of all believers, not just Catholics.[4] I remember telling my ten-year-old friend in Minnesota that it was a shame he couldn't go to heaven because he was not a Catholic, which was the "one true Church."

FROM CONFLICT TO COLLABORATION

A lot has changed in American religion and politics since 1960. One of the most significant changes is the development of a surprising, complicated, and positive relationship between evangelical and Catholic leaders in advancing their distinctive Christian visions as allies and sometimes partners in public life.

With increasing frequency, Catholic and evangelical leaders have come together to defend human life and dignity, to protect religious freedom and promote family life, and to pursue justice and peace. Evangelical and Catholic leaders serve different communities with contrasting histories, theological beliefs, political perspectives, partisan affiliations, and ethnic and economic backgrounds. As a result, when they work together

---

3. Papers of John F. Kennedy. Pre-Presidential Papers. Presidential Campaign Files, 1960. Religious Issue Files of James Wine, 1960. Religious literature: National Association of Evangelicals.

4. Paul VI, Vatican II *Dignitas Humanae: On the Right of the Person and of Communities to Social and Civil Freedom in Matters Religious*, December 7, 1965.

they do so with differing sources of authority, contrasting styles, distinctive structures, and overlapping but not identical priorities.

FOCUS AND BACKGROUND

In this essay, I share my own experience and reflections drawn from collaboration with Catholic and evangelical leaders on issues of social, economic, environmental ,and global justice. There are many other important issues and elements in the broader relationship of Catholics and evangelicals. I also focus primarily on the efforts of institutional leadership in both communities, specifically the United States Conference of Catholic Bishops (USCCB) and the National Association of Evangelicals (NAE). I draw on their key statements, especially the several versions of *Forming Consciences for Faithful Citizenship*,[5] developed and adopted by the USCCB, and *For the Health of the Nation*,[6] developed and adopted by the NAE.

These examples of significant organizational collaboration are only a part of a broader picture of Catholics and evangelicals working together in public life. Often, particular elements within each community come together around specific issues or leaders. For example, Sojourners and Catholic social justice leaders work together on poverty, racism, and immigration issues. Some Catholic pro-life organizations and the "moral majority" have worked together on abortion. Evangelicals for Social Action and Catholic leaders helped found the National Religious Partnership for the Environment. A number of evangelical and Catholic leaders joined in the *Manhattan Declaration*[7] on religious freedom and an earlier formal statement *Catholics and Evangelicals Together* led by Fr. Richard John Neuhaus and Charles Colson.[8]

In this essay, I share my personal perspectives on this growing relationship and some of its elements and impacts, drawing on my own limited experience and past presentations I have made to Catholics and evangelicals

5. United States Conference of Catholic Bishops, *Forming Consciences for Faithful Citizenship: A Call to Political Responsibility from the Catholic Bishops of the United States*, November 2015.

6. National Association of Evangelicals, *For the Health of the Nation: An Evangelical Call to Civic Responsibility*, 2004.

7. Robert George, Timothy George, Chuck Colson, "Manhattan Declaration," Manhattan Declaration Inc., November 20, 2009.

8. Various, "Evangelicals and Catholics Together: The Christian Mission in the Third Millennium," *First Things*, May 1994.

over the years. I do not offer original research, groundbreaking analysis, or deep theological insight, but rather some modest directions, dangers, and lessons I have learned over two decades working with evangelical leaders to find common ground to advance the common good.

MISSION

In looking back, it is vital that leaders in both the Catholic and evangelical communities are clear about their mission and understanding of what their role in public life is and is not. We are communities of faith, not special interest groups. We draw our strength and direction from the Scriptures and our moral teaching, not from any political program or ideological agenda. In the old cliché, we are not the "Democratic Party at prayer," nor are we the "Religious Caucus of the Republican Party."

In *Forming Consciences for Faithful Citizenship*, the bishops describe the obligations and contributions of believers in public life:

> In the Catholic Tradition, responsible citizenship is a virtue and participation in political life is a moral obligation.[9]

> Our nation's tradition of pluralism is enhanced, not threatened, when religious groups and people of faith bring their convictions and concerns into public life. Indeed, our Church's teaching is in accord with the foundational values that have shaped our nation's history: "life, liberty, and the pursuit of happiness."[10]

The bishops cite a key contribution of Pope Benedict XVI:

> It is not the church's responsibility to make this teaching prevail in political life. Rather, the Church wishes to help form consciences in political life and to stimulate greater insight into the authentic requirements of justice as well as greater readiness to act accordingly, even when this might involve conflict with situations of personal interest.[11]

The best mission statement I have read is not in *Faithful Citizenship* or *For the Health of the Nation*, but in the Gospel of Luke where Jesus begins

---

9. *Forming Consciences for Faithful Citizenship*, USCCB, 13.

10. Ibid., 11.

11. Benedict XVI, *Deus Caritas Est*, 28.

his public life by reading a powerful passage from Isaiah which describes his mission on earth and our tasks today:

to bring good news to the poor,

liberty to captives,

recovery of sight to the blind,

to set free those who are oppressed (4:18).

CONTEXT

We carry out these tasks in a very challenging context and sometimes hostile environment. We try to "form consciences" in a very divided, increasingly secular nation where moral boundaries are flexible and self-interest and rampant individualism are powerful forces. We seek to bring "good news to the poor" in an economy that leaves millions behind and in a nation with massive gaps between rich and poor. We try to bring "liberty to captives" when many are imprisoned by discrimination and racism, mass incarceration and addiction. We try to bring "sight to the blind" in a culture where we can be blinded by partisanship, prejudice, or privilege, ideology or indifference. We are called to "set free those who are oppressed" in neighborhoods that lack work and hope, in a world haunted by hunger and despair, and at a time when believers' lives and freedoms are threatened because of their faith.

SIX ASSETS

In the face of these challenges, religious communities do bring traditional assets that make a difference in Washington. We do not offer political contributions or endorsements, though some religious leaders have unfortunately crossed these lines. Rather, we bring a different set of assets that are reflected in different ways and different strengths in evangelical and Catholic communities. In citing these assets, I mostly focus on the Catholic community since that is what I know best.

1. Biblical Foundations

The Scriptures obviously do not offer specific legislative or policy guidance, but the Word of God does offer foundations, directions, and priorities to guide the choices of believers in our lives, including our participation in public life. Evangelicals and Catholics treat and see the Bible in differing ways, with different interpretations and often with different levels of knowledge and authority. In my experience, evangelicals know more of the Bible, and are more ready to use scriptural references, and to make biblical arguments in the public forum than many Catholics.

2. Moral principles

The Catholic Church has developed, especially over the last 125 years, a body of formal Catholic Social Doctrine expressed in a long series of papal encyclicals and other official ecclesial documents.[12] These principles and their applications are at the center of Catholic analysis and advocacy on public policy. The USCCB offers statements, testimony, and letters explicitly using these principles as criteria for assessing, supporting, or opposing policies. This formal moral framework helps to keep Catholic participation in public life grounded, focused, consistent, and helps avoid the temptation to adapt Christian faith to reflect the ideological or policy fashions of the moment.

Evangelicals do not have a similar body of formal teaching, but often draw on some of these principles to shape their own analysis and advocacy. In ecumenical and interfaith efforts, the principles of Catholic Social Teaching are sometimes used to find common ground and unite different traditions in common advocacy. Ironically, I sometimes find more interest in and knowledge of Catholic Social Teaching among some evangelicals than among many Catholics.

3. Everyday Experience

In my work, the effectiveness of religious advocacy often depends more on what we do than what we believe or say. Our everyday experience in feeding the hungry, sheltering the homeless, caring for the sick, welcoming immigrants, fighting hunger and disease in the poorest places on earth brings credibility and persuasiveness to our public witness. In the Catholic community, these efforts are often more structured and organized through

12. Pontifical Council for Justice and Peace, *Compendium of the Social Doctrine of the Church,* 2004.

dioceses, Catholic Charities, Catholic school systems, Catholic hospitals, and other structures than in the evangelical community,

4. Presence, Structures, Institutions

By definition, the Catholic Church is a hierarchical institution led by the Pope, including formal ties of communion of local dioceses within a universal church, a national conference of bishops, and an elaborate structure of parishes, schools, and charities working within dioceses. There are also state Catholic conferences in almost forty states led by bishops to help coordinate Catholic policy efforts at the state level. These formal relationships can sometimes be more theoretical than real, but they do provide structures for ecclesial accountability, mutual support, and common effort. This is often helpful, but also a burden when there are institutional failures like the horrific sexual abuse crisis in the Catholic Church.

Obviously, the evangelical community is not structured in this way. Pastors and other leaders are less accountable to larger structures. This can make common commitments more difficult, but evangelical leaders can respond independently and quickly while Catholic leaders are bound by more elaborate structures of consultation and accountability which can take time and reduce flexibility. I have often said the USCCB can be a very useful ally, but it is not an easy partner because of its organizational processes, restrictions, and timelines.

5. People

In the Catholic community, the most important and underdeveloped resource is our people. There are more than 70 million Catholics across the United States. The Catholic Church is one of the few communities in American life that is bipartisan, multiracial, and multiethnic and crosses economic and ideological lines. We are urban, suburban, and rural; Democrats, Republicans, and Independents. Catholics are in the Senate and work in fields picking vegetables, own businesses and participate in labor unions. If Catholics could unite more effectively around our moral principles, we could have major impact. Unfortunately, for many Catholics, party and class, prejudice and self-interest can be more powerful factors than our common faith in how we act as citizens and voters. The evangelical community shares some of these challenges and qualities, but has different regional presence, economic profile, ethnic and racial make-up, and partisan affiliations.

6. Leaders

Both communities are blessed with extraordinary leaders and many leadership challenges. The leadership of the NAE, particularly President Leith Anderson and Vice President for Public Policy Galen Carey, are deeply committed to collaboration with Catholics in these areas. I have also been honored to work with Rev. Jim Wallis of Sojourners and Ron Sider of Evangelicals for Social Action on connecting Catholics and evangelicals on issues of economic, environmental, and social justice. Bread for the World and ecumenical and interfaith coalitions bring evangelicals and Catholic leaders together with others to pursue common goals.

A unique asset for the Catholic community is the papacy, which is a source of unity, visibility, authority, and direction. Pope John Paul II and Pope Benedict XVI in different ways and in different times provided bold witness, clear teaching, and powerful leadership. John Paul II was in many ways the pope of solidarity and his witness helped free millions in Eastern Europe and beyond. Pope Benedict XVI is underappreciated as a teacher of Catholic social principles and a leader in placing care for creation at the center of Catholic life.

Pope Francis, in his strong words and humble ways, is an extraordinary source of unity, urgency, and mission not only for Catholics, but also for other Christians and people of goodwill. His priority for the poor; his defense of the unborn, the young, and the old; his welcome for immigrants and refugees; his pleas for religious freedom and peace; and his call to care for God's creation offer elements of a common path forward. Pope Francis looks at the economy, the world, and the church from the bottom up and from the outside in. He warns against a "throwaway culture" and calls for love in family life, justice in economic life, dialogue in political life, and mercy in ecclesial life. Before he became pope and now as the leader of the Catholic Church, Francis has reached out to evangelical leaders and communities to strengthen ties and call for common action. As one evangelical leader said, "You have a Pope who knows how to pope."

27

CONTRASTS

Beyond difference in structure and demographics, theology and ecclesiology, there are other contrasts in how Catholic and evangelical leaders address issues in public life. Generalizations can oversimplify, but they can also enlighten. Catholics and evangelicals often differ in their view of government, with many Catholics more clear about its responsibilities and many evangelicals more aware of its limitations. Catholic social teaching upholds and advocates institutions with global authority and many evangelicals can be skeptical of the United Nations and similar institutions. I have found that Catholic leaders are less inclined than evangelicals to link the mission of charity and the duty to evangelize.

There have also been differences over the use of the death penalty, moral justification for the use of military force, and the pursuit of a just peace in the Holy Land. Probably for reasons of history, I find Catholic leaders are more committed to the role of unions and community organizing than their evangelical counterparts. There can also be differences over the wisdom and limits of interfaith and ecumenical collaboration.

SIX LESSONS

In carrying out this mission in this challenging context, here are several lessons based on my particular and limited experience:

1. Religious policy advocacy needs to be distinctive, clearly reflecting biblical values, religious principles, and the experience of religious communities in its language, tone, and topics. Partisan rhetoric, ideological talking points and political threats are neither helpful nor appropriate.

    Sometimes, individual statements from key religious leaders and/or organizations can have greater impact than more generic sign-on letters of many religious voices. There are times, however, when a common statement from a broad and diverse coalition of religious leaders can communicate extraordinary unity, strength, and common purpose.

2. The church is often better at shaping fundamental questions, offering moral criteria, and lifting up the human dimensions of public issues than defining policy specifics of how to address these challenges. It is

often easier to be more clear on what choices, policies, and directions should be avoided than on specific details or technical elements of what policies should be adopted. How public questions are framed can be decisive in how they are answered. Here are three examples:

- The principles of Just War teaching helped to shape debates about US intervention in Iraq. Questions of just cause, right authority, last resort, and proportionality were at the center of debate. Sadly, the warnings of Pope John Paul II and the questions of the US bishops were ignored and overridden and our country and the people of Iraq have paid a terrible price.

- In the case of the HHS Mandate on contraceptive coverage, I found that when the focus was on whether the federal government should define what is a religious ministry or whether religious organizations should be forced to act against their moral teaching, religious freedom advocates gained ground. When the focus shifted to whether private employers can deny contraception coverage to their employees because of employers' religious or moral convictions, religious freedom advocates lost ground. It did not help that an early and very visible Congressional hearing on this matter began with a panel of five male clerics and no women. Questions matter and so do symbols.

- One of the most remarkable achievements of Catholic and evangelical witness has been the defense of the lives of unborn children when so many powerful forces in media, politics, and culture opposed our efforts over five decades. As others have pointed out, when the question is *what* is done (i.e., destruction of an unborn child), pro-life arguments are more likely to prevail. When the question is *who* decides (i.e., a woman or government), pro-choice advocates often prevail. This may be why we have been described as both an anti-abortion nation and pro-choice society.

There are times when religious advocacy not only helps define key questions, but also contributes to important policy achievements. In past years, these accomplishments have included the Partial Birth Abortion Ban and family and medical leave; third world debt relief and the International Religious Freedom Act and Commission; the Earned Income Tax Credit and the Refundable Children's Tax Credit; and funding and improvement of poverty-focused development assistance, action on human trafficking, and preserving and strengthening the safety net and children's health care.

3. Another lesson is that intense *political and ideological polarization in our nation is also distorting Christian witness and damaging ecclesial life.* Especially among elites, there is a terrible temptation to misuse faith, Scripture, and church teaching as talking points for narrow ideological preferences or partisan choices. There are organized factions in both communities that selectively apply our values and principles to support particular political platforms or preferred candidates, rather than testing policies, parties, and politicians by the values of the gospel and the consistent criteria of church teaching.

Too often, campaigns and elections bring out the worst of us, exacerbating divisions, increasing harsh rhetoric, and destroying unity and consistency in the community of faith. A key question for all of us is "does your faith shape your politics, or does your politics shape your faith?"

In my view, Catholic and evangelical contributions to public life can be undermined when some religious progressives minimize or excuse Democratic orthodoxy which opposes any and all restrictions on abortion, or some religious conservatives ignore or excuse Republican policies that threaten the poor or demonize immigrants and refugees. Religious leaders need to challenge the growing libertarianism of left and right that make either "personal choice" or the "free market" the measure of everything, leaving little room for the defense of the unborn or undocumented, a priority for the poor or the common good.

4. *"Political homelessness"* can be an accurate description of where consistent-ethic Catholics and some evangelicals find themselves, but it is also a reflection of our inability to persuade others to share the principles and priorities which we bring to the public square. Political homelessness is not a badge of honor, sign of political purity, or call to abandon or denigrate political life. Instead it is a challenge to engage and persuade our neighbors, fellow citizens, and political leaders to share a consistent commitment to human life and dignity. If someone is homeless, they need to find a shelter or home. We need to work to build places, perhaps caucuses, in both parties for believers and members who share a common commitment to human life *and* human dignity, rights *and* responsibilities, solidarity *and* subsidiarity, care for

creation *and* the common good. We need more, not less, principled participation in our political parties and public life.

5. The teaching, preaching, and witness of evangelical ministers and Catholic bishops and priests are essential in bringing the values of the gospel into public debate and decisions. However, these ecclesial obligations are not a substitute for the *active and engaged, principled and informed participation of lay women and men in our politics.* This is a central part of the mission of our Initiative on Catholic Social Thought and Public Life at Georgetown University: to help lay Catholics, especially young people, to become "salt, light and leaven" in our communities and nation.

6. *We will not change our politics without changing our culture* on fundamental matters of life and death, care for the weak and vulnerable. We may be able to prevail on some issues, but to make a real and lasting difference we have to change the way large segments of our society think about human life and dignity. In our nation, life is often cheap and people are treated as things. Catholic and evangelical leaders will not prevail until we persuade our fellow citizens to not see the unborn child as an imposition, the elderly as burdens, immigrants and refugees as threats, torture as necessary, criminals as animals, civilian casualties as collateral damage, and the hungry of the world as someone else's problem. We must find ways to resist what Pope Francis calls a "throwaway culture."[13]

FOUR DIRECTIONS AND DANGERS

Based on *Faithful Citizenship,* I have offered some directions and dangers for institutional evangelical and Catholic leaders on their opportunities, responsibilities, and limitations in public life. For moral, political, and ecclesial reasons, I believe our distinctive approaches and common efforts need to be:

1. **Political, not partisan:** Catholic and evangelical leaders need to lift up the moral and human dimensions of political issues. We need to apply the values of Scripture and principles of our teaching to public choices since these are matters of life and death, human dignity and

13. "Pope Decries 'Throwaway culture,' Calls for Generational Solidarity," *Vatican Radio,* June 16, 2014.

solidarity, and justice and peace. However, we should not be chaplain to any party, cheerleader for any candidate, apologist for any administration. No party and few candidates represent a clear and consistent reflection of the moral message of our communities. The identification of the gospel or the body of Christ with a particular party is a form of idolatry and over time brings serious moral, ecclesial, and political damage.

2. **Principled, not ideological:** Christian leaders are required to apply the values of Scripture and the principles of our faith to public issues. We should not abandon our moral principles, but we should work with others who share our goals, but not necessarily our faith or all our convictions. We should not mistake differences in priorities or tactics for disagreement on fundamental principles. Seeking the common good requires working across partisan, ideological, and religious lines and often the need for compromise. In Mark Shields's insightful words, "you can tell the health of a movement, party . . . or church . . . by whether they are looking for heretics or converts." We are in the conversion business.

3. **Civil, not soft:** Catholic and evangelical leaders should state our convictions clearly. We cannot abandon the unborn, the unemployed, or immigrants and refugees, or turn away from promotion of family life or care for creation. However, our witness is not advanced by challenging the motives of others, by impugning their faith, integrity, or character. Christians who work for greater justice, charity, and respect in our society must practice these virtues in our public life. We need to engage and persuade others with our ideas, our experience, our people, and the hope and love that comes with faith. None of this is advanced by name-calling, threats, or intimidation.

4. **Engaged, not used:** Evangelical and Catholic leaders cannot avoid or abandon public life because politics is where fundamental moral choices are made. However, we should engage in ways that reflect who we are and what we believe, not be used to advance narrow partisan causes or ideological agendas. We need to share our experience, values, and message, not pose for photo ops or serve as religious props in political settings. Our voice, message, and actions should be distinctive, reflecting the gospel and our teaching, not the polarization of our politics. We must make our case to our leaders, but in our ways and

hopefully in our own settings . . . at a soup kitchen, pregnancy center, or homeless shelter. We cannot trade access for authentic witness.

AN EXAMPLE: EVANGELICAL–CATHOLIC LEADERSHIP SUMMIT ON OVERCOMING POVERTY

There have been many examples of evangelical-Catholic cooperation at local and national levels. One of the most formal and focused was the *Evangelical-Catholic Leadership Summit on Overcoming Poverty* in May of 2015, cosponsored by NAE and the Initiative on Catholic Social Thought and Public Life at Georgetown University.

This unique effort brought together for three days almost 200 diverse evangelical and Catholic leaders as well as key policymakers, researchers, and other religious and community leaders. This Summit explicitly sought to move beyond religious, ideological, and partisan boundaries. It included both those who see family factors and those who emphasize economic factors as primary causes and remedies for poverty. In the most visible of many dialogues, the Summit brought President Barack Obama, Harvard professor Robert Putnam, and American Enterprise Institute President Arthur Brooks together in an unprecedented panel seeking common ground in overcoming poverty. But they were not alone: leaders of Sojourners and Focus on the Family were joined by Catholic leaders from Nuns on the Bus and Opus Dei programs, Senators Tim Scott and Cory Booker, leaders of business and labor, progressive and conservative researchers, and advocates in a unique model of evangelical-Catholic collaboration.

The momentum of the Summit contributed to the essential and ongoing work of the *Circle of Protection,* which was founded by Catholic, evangelical, and other Christian leaders to protect programs that serve "the least of these" in federal budget debate and decisions. In past years, the ecumenical leadership of the Circle met with President Obama, Representative Paul Ryan, and other leaders to safeguard the domestic safety net and international anti-poverty and hunger programs. It is working with renewed urgency and focus to protect those who are sick, hungry, and poor in today's chaotic and threatening policy and political environment.

CONCLUSION

Fifty years after the NAE pamphlet warning about "the Church of Rome" and a Catholic President in 1960, Leith Anderson and Galen Carey, president and vice president of the NAE, were invited to meet with the USCCB's committees on domestic and international policy to discuss, strategize, and celebrate common efforts to protect and enhance human life and dignity.

Toward the end of the discussion, I sought to remind the Committees of the distance we had traveled as two Christian communities with historic differences and distrust to work closely and collaboratively on issues of life and family and on the challenges of poverty and peace, religious freedom, and immigration, care for creation, and global development. The president of the NAE smiled and said something like "Yeah, it's good you guys got on board." We all laughed and thanked God we have found important ways to work together to share the good news of the gospel and its implications for public policy. Only friends and allies can laugh about the ways two very different Christian communities have come together after decades of distance and even past hostility.

We have come a long way from the mutual suspicion and distrust of 1960. In a 2014 survey, US evangelical leaders unanimously supported co-operation between evangelicals and Catholics on social and public policy issues of mutual concern.[14] On a wide range of issues, the United States Conference of Catholic Bishops looks to evangelical leaders and organizations as one of its most consistent allies and partners.

At this time of new threats to poor families and communities, intense political polarization, and growing national, racial, and ideological divisions, this Catholic-evangelical relationship is more important than ever as we seek in our own ways and in common efforts to "to bring "good news to the poor, liberty to captives, recovery of sight to the blind, to set free those who are oppressed" (Luke 4:18).

14. "Evangelical Leaders Survey: Cooperation with Catholics," nae.net.

4

Lessons To Be Learned from the Political Engagement of Evangelicals and Catholics: An Evangelical Perspective

Stephen V. Monsma

I BEGIN THIS ESSAY with four quotations, two of which are from the 2004 official statement of the National Association of Evangelicals (NAE) entitled, *For the Health of the Nation: An Evangelical Call to Civic Responsibility*, and two of which are from the 2007 statement of the United States Conference Catholic of Bishops (USCCB) entitled, *Forming Consciences for Faithful Citizenship*, which was reissued by the Bishops in 2011.

> The vulnerable [about whom God cares deeply] may include not only the poor, but women, children, the aged, persons with disabilities, immigrants, refugees, minorities, the persecuted, and the prisoners. God measures societies by how they treat the people at the bottom.[1]

> A basic moral test for our society is how we treat the most vulnerable in our midst. . . . Scripture gives us the story of the Last

---

1. *For the Health of the Nation: An Evangelical Call to Civic Responsibility* (Washington, DC: National Association of Evangelicals Office for Governmental Affairs, 2004), 18.

> Judgment (see Mt 25:31–46) and reminds us that we will be judged
> by our response to the "least among us."[2]

> Because God created human beings in his image, we are endowed
> with rights and responsibilities.[3]

> Corresponding to these rights are duties and responsibilities—to
> one another, to our families, and to the larger society.[4]

I challenge any one to say which are from the evangelical document and which are from the Catholic document. My point is, of course, that there is enormous convergence between evangelical and Catholic positions and concerns in the public policy arena.

Perhaps this is an instance of the old saying that politics makes for strange bedfellows. However—and I cannot emphasize this too strongly— the convergence between evangelicals and Catholics runs much deeper than a "strange bedfellows" pragmatic agreement on certain public policy questions of the day such as abortion, same-sex marriage, and euthanasia. Instead, it is rooted in a worldview and a perspective shaped by Scripture and by our Lord and Savior whom we together acknowledge and worship. It is based on common beliefs involving the dignity and worth of all human beings, the God-created and God-intended centrality of the family in God's ordering of society, a commitment to seeking the common good that is much more than the adjustment of competing private interests, and the moral responsibility all human beings have both as individuals and as members of society.

In preparation for writing this paper I read the various documents associated with the "Evangelicals and Catholics Together" efforts of the past twelve or fifteen years. What emerged is the fact that as we have talked together we have come to see that in spite of certain real differences, our agreements are more and more basic than our disagreements. As the original 1994 "Evangelicals and Catholics Together" document stated: "In the exercise of these public responsibilities there has been a growing convergence and cooperation between Evangelicals and Catholics."[5]

---

2. *Forming Consciences for Faithful Citizenship: A Call to Political Responsibility from the Catholic Bishops of the United States* (Washington, DC: United States Conference of Catholic Bishops, 2007), 14.

3. *For the Health of the Nation*, 21.

4. *Forming Consciences for Faithful Citizenship*, 14.

5. "ECT Statement: 'Evangelicals and Catholics Together: The Christian Mission in

Once when I met for breakfast with a Catholic priest, we discussed evangelical-Catholic agreement on many public policy issues and the priest suggested that if a group of evangelicals and a group of Catholics were both meeting in the same restaurant for breakfast one morning to lay plans for influencing the public policy direction of their city or state, and if someone came in late, and by mistake sat at the wrong table, it would probably be a half hour before this person figured out that he had joined the wrong group! As the evangelical historian, Mark Noll, and his collaborator, Carolyn Nystrom, have written: "Especially on pro-life and pro-family questions, the difficult thing to imagine now is how evangelicals and Catholics could ever have been at odds."[6]

A PARADOX

Yet, a paradox exists, a paradox that I believe ought to shame Catholics and evangelicals alike: namely, our agreement on public policy perspectives and goals is much greater than our level of cooperation and coordination. What Richard John Neuhaus wrote in broader terms certainly applies to the public policy realm: "The problem, indeed, the scandal, is that we are united but live as though we were not."[7]

In writing this paper I have struggled to gain an accurate picture of the nature and extent of evangelical-Catholic cooperation and coordination on public policy issues. It has not been easy. On the one hand collaboration is clearly present. For example, in March, 2012, in response to certain cultural trends and several actions of the Obama administration a large number of prominent Catholics and Evangelicals issued a joint statement "as brothers and sisters in Christ" entitled, "In Defense of Religious Liberty."[8] On the passage of the 1998 International Religious Freedom Act (IRFA) political scientist and widely recognized expert on religious free-

---

the Third Millennium," Charles Colson and Richard John Neuhaus, eds., *Evangelicals and Catholics Together: Toward a Common Mission* (Dallas, TX: Word, 1995), xxii. Also see in this volume the essays by Charles Colson and George Weigel.

6. Mark A. Noll and Carolyn Nystrom, *Is the Reformation Over? An Evangelical Assessment of Contemporary Roman Catholicism* (Grand Rapids: Baker, 2005), 20. Later these authors highlight areas of evangelical-Catholic agreement in the areas of respect for human life, sexual ethics, family and marriage, and social justice. See 125–29.

7. Richard John Neuhaus, "The Catholic Difference," in Colson and Neuhaus, eds., *Evangelicals and Catholics Together*, 187. Italics removed.

8. See "In Defense of Religious Liberty," *First Things* (March, 2012).

dom, Alan Hertzke, reports that Catholics, evangelicals, and Jews were all actively involved in the passage of this act that has done much for the cause of religious freedom around the world.[9] Nina Shea, a Catholic, and Paul Marshall, an evangelical, were keys persons at Freedom House who teamed up to get the word out on the scandal of religious persecution in many parts of the world.[10] Galen Carey, the vice president for public affairs of the National Association of Evangelicals, has reported that the public affairs staff of the United States Conference of Catholic Bishops and he work closely together on various public policy issues: "There are at least a dozen people at the Catholic Conference that I have regular contact with . . . The Catholic Conference is probably our closest allies as compared to mainline denominations—more than with other Protestants."[11] Catholic and evangelical scholars work together on public policy issues and questions at the Washington-based Ethics and Public Policy Center. The Family Research Council—which grew out of James Dobson's evangelical-oriented Focus on the Family—has a number of prominent Catholics on its staff and board. Michael Moses of the general council office of the USCCB has been a member of the board of the Institutional Religious Freedom Alliance (IRFA), an organization largely composed of evangelicals.

And yet, I come away with the impression that this is not the entire story. Something is missing. Given our agreements on both specific public policy issues and priorities and, more importantly, given our agreement on theological and worldview perspectives that underlie those agreements, one comes away thinking there should be more cooperation and coordination of efforts than there are. Most current efforts at cooperation and coordination appear to be informal, ad hoc, and individual, rather than formalized, ongoing, and institutionalized. Too often we charge off on our own without consulting our brothers and sisters in Christ across the Catholic-evangelical boundary. The glass of Catholic-evangelical collaboration in public policy advocacy is half full; it is also half empty.

Richard Cizik, the former vice president for governmental affairs for the National Association of Evangelicals, reports that in his time with the NAE he took part in many coalitions in support of various causes—such

---

9. See Allen D. Hertzke, *Freeing God's Children: The Unlikely Alliance for Global Human Rights* (Lanham, MD: Rowman & Littlefield, 2004), 193–201.

10. See Hertzke's account of the contribution of these two persons in raising the visibility of the religious persecution issue. Ibid., 119–128.

11. Telephone interview with Galen Carey (September 4, 2012).

as sex trafficking, religious persecution, and global climate change—and various groups were involved in regular meetings to plan strategies and to coordinate activities.[12] But he reports Catholics were not involved as an organized entity. Earlier I related that Hertzke has reported Catholic involvement in the passage of IRFA, yet in a telephone interview with me Hertzke, who is himself Catholic, also reported that Catholics were not, as Cizik also told me, a part of the group that met regularly to plan strategy and coordinate action.[13] He reported that Catholics indeed supported the legislation and were actively involved in winning its passage, publicly endorsing it and making key phone calls in support of it. But USCCB representatives did not work closely with evangelicals and other groups who were meeting regularly for strategy sessions and working day in and day out for its passage.

Similarly, evangelical advocacy groups—with their splintered nature that spans the political spectrum—regularly tackle public policy questions and seek to drum up support for their causes with little or no thought to listening to and coordinating their activities with their Catholic brothers and sisters. In March 2012, for example, the Evangelical Immigration Table put out an "Evangelical Statement of Principles for Immigration Reform" that was signed by what reads like a Who's Who in the evangelical world.[14] Catholics were notable by their absence—because they were not consulted or asked to participate, even though various Catholic statements closely parallel the statement of the Evangelical Immigration Table.[15] In any given

12. Telephone interview with Richard Cizik (April 11, 2008).

13. Telephone interview with Allen D. Hertzke (April 15, 2008).

14. See Evangelical Immigration Table, "Evangelical Statement of Principles for Immigration Reform." Available at http://evangelicalimmigrationtable.com.

15. The fact that Catholics were not asked to join this effort was confirmed to me in an email dated November 6, 2012 by Galen Carey, the vice president for public affairs of the NAE. Carey, however, also pointed out that the evangelicals felt they needed to get the broad spectrum of evangelical groups together on the same page before seeking to cooperate with others. He also pointed out that he and other evangelicals have been working with the USCCB and other allies on the immigration issue and that they are indeed "coordinating closely with them." On the two traditions being close together on immigration reform, the earlier referenced document, *Forming Consciences for Faithful Citizenship*, reads, "The Gospel mandate to 'welcome the stranger' requires Catholics to care for and stand with immigrants, both documented and undocumented . . ." (para. 83) and the Evangelical Immigration Table's statement reads, "As evangelical Christian leaders, we call for a bipartisan solution on immigration that: Respects the God-given dignity of every person, Protects the unity of the immediate family. . . . Establishes a path toward legal status and/or citizenship for those who qualify and who wish to become permanent residents."

case, as here, one can make an argument in favor of either evangelicals or Catholics acting alone, but I believe it happens all too often.

In short, the coordination and cooperation between the two huge Christian traditions in the United States that most closely share theological and worldview perspectives remain limited and ad hoc.

REASONS FOR LIMITED COORDINATION AND COOPERATION

This leads to the question of why there has not been greater and more formal working together by evangelicals and Catholics on public policy issues. Part of the answer lies in the nature of evangelical public policy engagement in recent years. It was only since about 1980 that evangelicals have burst onto the national scene as significant players in the electoral and public policy advocacy fields. I am thinking here of Jerry Falwell and Moral Majority, Pat Robertson and the Christian Coalition, James Dobson and Focus on the Family. And we often made a mess of it. Without a strong tradition of social teaching and no church authority to rein in the more exuberant and unwise among us, we all too often pursued an overly narrow, conservative, partisan agenda. We advocated policy positions on issues of concern for the poor and on war and peace that sounded more like the right wing of the Republican Party than biblically informed positions. We ended up time and again being used, as Cal Thomas has put it, as a "cheap date" by Republican Party operatives more skillful and cynical than we.[16] Thomas has also described our tendency to rush into complex public policy issues with a minimum of thought as a practice of: "Ready, fire, aim!"[17] Given potential public policy allies such as these, a hesitancy on the part of Catholic public policy advocacy groups, such as the Government Relations office of the USCCB, is understandable and perhaps even commendable. And Evangelical groups were often too eager to rush into the political fray to bother with seeking allies among Catholic leaders and organizations.

Closely related to this fact of evangelical public policy advocacy is the host of evangelical advocacy groups. We are a fractured, contentious lot. I

16. Cal Thomas, in Cal Thomas and Ed Dobson, *Blinded by Might: Why the Religious Right Can't Save America* (Grand Rapids: Zondervan, 1999), 143–44.

17. I first heard Thomas make this comment at a conference at Wheaton College many years ago and I have come across it in other of his writings, but I have not been able to locate those writings nor do I recall the date of the conference where I first heard it.

can imagine Catholic public policy advocates who wish to work with evangelicals in public policy advocacy shaking their heads in dismay as they try to figure out with whom they should partner.

Both the overly narrow, uniformly conservative agenda of many evangelical organizations—and especially the largest of them—and the multiplicity of evangelical advocacy organizations stand in contrast to the USCCB, with its long history of thoughtful, balanced policy positions, its access to key persons in positions of power in Washington built up over long years of advocacy, and its ability to speak with a united voice. Thus it is not surprising that the USCCB has become used to moving ahead on its own in its advocacy efforts.

But let me dig a bit deeper. This is not the whole story. There is also at times a matter of differences of priorities and strategies rooted in our two traditions' different experiences. Let me use as an example, the public policy area with which I am most acquainted: the question of President Bush's faith-based initiative and the charitable choice provision that was added to the 1996 welfare reform act and later to other legislation. These efforts were aimed at assuring that faith-based social service organizations were free to compete on a level playing field for government money funding of nonprofit social service programs and at protecting both persons receiving those services from violations of their religious freedom and the programs from having to jettison their religious character.[18] Although there has been evangelical-Catholic cooperation on this issue and although the first two directors of the White House Office of Faith-Based and Community Initiatives were Catholics (John DiIulio and Jim Towey), there have also been misunderstandings and a lack of coordination between evangelicals and Catholics.

At the heart of these missteps lie different evangelical and Catholic approaches to this issue, even while there is agreement on principles and goals. Most evangelicals have learned to be suspicious of government and fearful of government control. We are not used to partnering with government and tend to feel weak and vulnerable when it comes to interacting with government. Thus when the question of government funding for our social service agencies comes up, we tend to be suspicious. We are increasingly willing to partner with government, but we feel a bit like we are riding

18. The following discussion is based on my own observations and discussions with Stanley Carlson-Thies of the Center for Public Justice and now the Coalition for Institutional Religious Freedom.

on the back of a tiger, and to avoid ending up inside we want some firm guarantees and written assurances that government is not going to interfere with our religious mission. My impression is that Catholics are less fearful of government, both due to a less anti-government tradition than that of many evangelicals and due to a longer history of working with and cooperating with government, usually on the local level. Catholic Charities has for some time worked out a *modus operandi* with government funding agencies, where accommodations have been made on both sides, often informally and without clearly written principles. This is a more pragmatic, let's-muddle-through approach than we evangelicals are comfortable with.

As a result, when evangelicals push for charitable choice legislation that clearly outlines the protections and rights of their organizations that receive government funding, Catholics may feel we are stirring up trouble unnecessarily. They may even feel evangelical efforts are counterproductive as groups opposed to government funding of faith-based programs are stirred into action and perhaps friendly legislators (often Catholic Democrats) are forced to take public stands that might cost them votes in the next election. The difference is not a difference of goals or principles; it is a difference in tactics and approaches, rooted in our different histories and assumptions.

THE POSSIBILITY AND NEED FOR CHANGE

I believe these differences can and need to be overcome. First, why I believe they can be overcome. From an evangelical perspective my optimism rests in the fact that the old evangelical right of the Moral Majority and the Christian Coalition is passing from the scene and is being replaced by a more thoughtful, nuanced, biblically based approach to public issues. There are numerous signs of a new wind blowing through the evangelical world that is placing new issues on the evangelical political agenda and leading many evangelicals to take centrist positions on them. In so doing we are moving closer to where Catholics, represented by the USCCB, have been all along.

As evidence of this trend I can point to the 2005 book, *Towards an Evangelical Public Policy,* a collection of essays that takes a thoroughly biblical, thoughtful approach to today's public policy issues. The document I referred to earlier in this paper, *For the Health of the Nation,* grew out of this larger volume. I could multiply similar examples almost indefinitely. There is the Evangelical Climate Initiative that warned against global warming and was signed by key evangelical leaders, including the presidents of Wheaton, Gordon, and Calvin Colleges, the editor of *Christianity Today*, the president of the Council of Christian Colleges and Universities, and such well-known evangelicals as Bill Hybels of Willow Creek Community Church and Rick Warren of Saddleback Church. In 2009 the NAE adopted a thoughtful, balanced resolution on immigration reform that calls, among other things, for a path to legal status for undocumented immigrants. The current vice president for government relations of the National Association of Evangelicals, Galen Carey, takes a thoughtful, centrist approach to public policy issues. There are rising Evangelical leaders such as Gabe Lyon, author of *The Next Christians* and founder of the organization, Q, which seeks "to mobilize Christians to advance the common good in society."[19] The 2008 presidential election year saw no less than six evangelical books, all of which reflect on and strengthen this emerging trend in the Evangelical world.[20] The president of World Vision, Richard Stearns, has written a well-received book entitled *The Hole in Our Gospel: What Does God Expect of Us?* that calls evangelicals to take a more active concern with problems of poverty and other social issues.[21]

These changes in the evangelical world lead me to conclude that we evangelicals and Catholic groups, and the USCCB in particular, may feel freer to partner together in a more formalized, institutionalized way than in the past. Especially the government affairs office of the NAE is a broadly

19. Gabe Lyon, *The Next Christians: Seven Ways You Can Live the Gospel and Restore the World* (Colorado Springs, CO: Multnomah, 2010). The quotation is from the back cover of the book.

20. See Amy E. Black, *Beyond Left and Right: Helping Christians Make Sense of American Politics* (Grand Rapids: Baker, 2008), Michael J. Gerson, *Heroic Conservatism: Why Republicans Need to Embrace America's Ideals* (New York: Harper, 2008), David P. Gushee, *The Future of Faith in American Politics: The Public Witness of the Evangelical Center* (Waco, TX: Baylor University Press, 2008), Brian D. McLaren, *Everything Must Change: Jesus, Global Crises, and a Revolution of Hope* (Nashville: Thomas Nelson, 2008), Ronald J. Sider, *The Scandal of Evangelical Politics: Why Are Christians Missing the Chance to Really Change the World* (Grand Rapids: Baker, 2008), and my own Stephen V. Monsma, *Healing for a Broken World: Christian Perspectives on Public Policy* (Wheaton, IL: Crossway, 2008). Also see the 2011 collection of thoughtful essays by evangelical scholars: David K. Ryden, ed., *Is the Good Book Good Enough? Evangelical Perspectives on Public Policy* (Lanham, MD: Lexington Books, 2011).

21. Richard E. Stearns, *The Hole in Our Gospel: What Does God Expect of Us? The Answer That Changed My Life and Might Just Change the World* (Seattle, WA: World Vision, 2009).

based, responsible, thoughtful peak association that would seem to be a natural for cooperation and collaboration with the public affairs office of the USCCB.

I am also convinced that greater Evangelical-Catholic cooperation and coordination are more crucial to achieve than ever before. When one reads the Evangelical statement I have referred to earlier, *For the Health of the Nation*, and reads *Forming Consciences for Faithful Citizenship* put out by the USCCB, one is struck not only by their similarities as I noted earlier, but also by something much less encouraging, namely, that the policy positions they advocate are almost the mirror image of the current policy trajectory in our nation. They assert human life is precious and abortion and embryonic stem cell research are to be avoided; abortion on demand continues unabated and the rush is on to embrace embryonic stem cell research. The movement towards same-sex marriage is opposed by both; the 2015 Supreme Court decision of *Obergefell v. Hodges* authorized same-sex marriages. The cause of the poor is upheld, but what candidate for public office dares to speak up for more generous policies to help the poor? Both documents advocate careful stewardship of God's creation; in our society economic concerns usually seem to trump environmental protection. Both call for just treatment and opportunities for legal status for undocumented immigrant workers; our politicians compete to sound the harshest in the treatment of undocumented immigrants.

I do not want to sound overly pessimistic, but we need to face facts. On issue after issue, the positions on which evangelicals and Catholics are articulating common responses are being ignored or opposed by the majority of our public office holders, would-be public office holders, and fellow citizens. This would be understandable if our two religious traditions were only a small percentage of the population. But the exact opposite is the case. The authoritative 2007 Pew Religious Landscape Survey reported that 26 percent of adult Americans are members of evangelical Protestant churches and another 24 percent are members of Roman Catholic churches.[22] If one adds evangelicals who attend either historically black churches or mainline Protestant churches, Catholics and evangelicals constitute a majority or—if one discounts for nominal members—a near majority of the population. However, our influence on the public policies of our nation is nowhere commensurate with our numbers.

22. See http://religions.pewforum.org/affiliations.

44

To me the lesson is clear: if we are to make a difference in our country, if the voice of biblical justice is to be heard, if solidarity and a commitment to the common good are to trump a selfish individualism, if families, our Christian social services organizations, and other of our civil society organizations are to be free to play a robust role in our society with their religious liberty rights intact, we need to work together.

SUGGESTIONS

I conclude this essay with three suggestions that I take away from what I have described in this paper. One is that we—evangelicals and Catholics—need to work more closely together in our efforts to influence the public policies our nation is pursuing and to do so on more issues. There is a basis for doing so. We agree on many specific issues and we largely agree on the biblical worldview perspectives and values that underlie our agreement on those specific issues. Also, there is an emerging center in the evangelical world—most clearly represented organizationally in the government affairs office of the National Association of Evangelicals—with whom the USCCB and especially its government relations office can work. This is already occurring, but more collaboration is needed. There is an opportunity here that only ten or fifteen years ago was not there. Also, the need to do so is clear. On issue after issue, we are losing, not gaining ground. In the name of the unborn, immigrants caught in our labyrinthian immigrant laws, the poor and imprisoned, threatened families, faith-based organizations threatened by a loss of their religious liberties, and HIV/AIDS sufferers around the world, we need to lay aside whatever differences of emphasis or tactics that divide us and join together in the work to which our Lord is calling us.

A second suggestion is a follow-up to the first: We need to develop structures and institutions within which we can carry on an ongoing discussion of public policy issues, the biblical worldview perspectives that underlie our understanding of public policy issues, and potential areas of cooperation and coordination. More specifically, I see the need, first, for a new public policy research center—a think tank—that is specifically designed to foster evangelical-Catholic dialogue and research. It would bring scholars and activists together from both traditions to explore our commonalities and differences, and to seek to expand our commonalities and foster joint initiatives. Second, I believe a coalition of evangelical and Catholic advocacy groups should meet regularly to plan strategy and coordinate activities on the public policy issues of the day. I see the Government Affairs Office of the NAE and the Government Relations Office of the USCCB potentially taking the lead on this, and by agreement inviting other organizations to join in these ongoing strategy and coordinating sessions.

A third suggestion emerges out of the challenges both Catholics and evangelicals face in overcoming a divide that threatens to exist between their public policy leadership and their average church members on public policy issues. The mainline Protestant churches are notorious for their church offices going off in their left-leaning direction, leaving their church members back in the dust someplace. Both Evangelicals and Catholics could succumb to the same danger. A national poll of either evangelicals or Catholics that would ask opinion questions based on the public policy positions advanced by the two documents I have cited at various points in this paper—the evangelical *For the Health of the Nation* and the Catholic *Forming Consciences for Faithful Citizenship*—might very well show a considerable gap between the leadership of both of our traditions and our everyday church members. I am convinced the lack of public policy success I mentioned earlier is in part due to less cooperation and coordination of efforts between Catholics and evangelicals than should be the case, but another cause may be that our ordinary church members are not following where our leaders are seeking to lead on public policy issues. This suggests to me that we both need to do a better job of educating and persuading our own members. And here also cooperative action may help.

Let me give an illustration from my personal experience. Back in 1972, in the pre-*Roe v. Wade* days, there was a referendum on the Michigan ballot that would have allowed abortion on demand during the first twenty weeks of pregnancy. The Sunday before the vote a Catholic parish priest whom I knew fairly well asked me to give the homily at all of the masses at his parish. I questioned why on earth he would want a Calvin College professor in the Reformed, evangelical tradition to speak. He replied that he felt many of his parishioners saw the abortion issue as just another Catholic issue. He felt that if a Protestant gave a similar message to the one he otherwise would give, it would be more effective. So I gave it a try. Although I am sure it was far from a great homily, I was deeply touched by how many who were in attendance expressed surprise and pleasure that of all persons a Calvin College professor was standing as one with them on the abortion issue.

There may be a lesson here. Perhaps the message Evangelical leaders such as Ron Sider, Galen Cary, Gabe Lyon, Michael Gerson, Rick Warren,

Richard Stearns, and others are working to bring to their fellow evangelicals would be made more powerful and persuasive, when their audience realizes this is not simply the message of a few evangelical leaders, but is the combined message of biblical Christians, Catholic and evangelical alike; and maybe the message the bishops and other Catholic leaders are working to bring to their fellow Catholics would be made more powerful and persuasive when their audience realizes this is not simply another Catholic message, but the combined witness of biblical Christians, Catholic and evangelical alike.

Peter Berger, the well know Boston University sociologist, once reportedly said that if India is the most religious country on earth and if Sweden is the most secular country on earth, the United States is a country of Indians ruled by Swedes![23] There is a majority, or near majority, of sincere, practicing evangelicals and Catholic voters in the United States, and one reason we are nevertheless being ruled by Swedes is due to our failure to realize more deeply and to live out more consistently our basic agreements. It is my prayer that the time, by God's grace, may be such that he is about to do a wondrous work of greater justice and peace in our land by bringing us together in political faithfulness.

23. I have heard this quotation of Peter Berger often mentioned, but have never been able to trace down a citation that gives its origin and conclusively shows its authenticity.

5

Forming Consciences for Faithful Citizenship: Underlying Philosophical, Theological, and Methodological Premises

JOHN BORELLI

INTRODUCTION

FOR FORTY YEARS, US Catholic bishops have offered formal guidance on good citizenship and prudent voting to the Catholic faithful of the United States. *Forming Consciences for Faithful Citizenship*, re-issued in 2015 with the subtitle *A Call to Political Responsibility from the Catholic Bishops of the United States with Introductory Note*, is the most recent version. The United States Conference of Catholic Bishops adopted this most recent, updated version at the bishops' November 2015 plenary meeting in preparation for the 2016 election year.

Forming Consciences states its intention in paragraph 5, as both an introductory statement and a clarification of purpose. The Catholic bishops of the United States wish to assist Catholics "to evaluate policy positions, party platforms, and candidates' promises and actions in light of the Gospel and the moral and social teaching of the Church in order to help build a better world."[1] In highlighting the role of the church in formation

1. United States Conference of Catholic Bishops, *Forming Consciences for Faithful*

48

of conscience and moral responsibility, the text draws from Scripture and tradition, offers principles, and lays out how these principles may apply to specific issues. The bishops urge Catholics to be prudent when deciding how to vote. Furthermore, paragraph 7 makes clear that the "bishops do not intend to tell Catholics for whom or against whom to vote." Hence, they advise that "the responsibility to make choices in political life rests with each individual in light of a properly formed conscience, and that participation goes well beyond casting a vote in a particular election." Good citizenship, prudence, and drawing from one's faith when making public decisions are all worthy values to promote.

These remarks on this hallmark statement of the US Catholic bishops derive from a presentation in September 2011 for an ongoing dialogue between evangelicals and Catholics. That dialogue, Catholics and Evangelicals for the Common Good, first met in March 2008 under sponsorship of Eastern University and its affiliated Palmer Theological Seminary, and Georgetown University. In that dialogue context, emphasis was required to illustrate how a major teaching document on public life by Catholic bishops draws from both Scripture and tradition, whose relationship had often been in dispute between Protestants and Catholics. Through the 1965 *Dogmatic Constitution on Divine Revelation* (*Dei Verbum* or "The Word of God"), the bishops of the Catholic Church worldwide, gathered at the Second Vatican Council, had sought to clarify this relationship:

> Hence sacred tradition and scripture are bound together in a close and reciprocal relationship. They both flow from the same divine wellspring, merge together to some extent, and are on course towards the same end. Scripture is the utterance of God as it is set down in writing under the guidance of God's Spirit; tradition preserves the word of God as it was entrusted to the apostles by Christ our lord and the holy Spirit, and transmits it to their successors, so that these in turn, enlightened by the Spirit of truth, may faithfully preserve, expound and disseminate the word by their preaching
> . . .
> Tradition and scripture together form a single sacred deposit of the word of God, entrusted to the church. (9–10)[2]

Citizenship: A Call to Political Responsibility from the Catholic Bishops of the United States with Introductory Note, http://www.usccb.org/issues-and-action/faithful-citizenship/upload/forming-consciences-for-faithful-citizenship.pdf. Hereafter, references to this 2015 text will be from the version on the USCCB website and often referred to simply as *Forming Consciences*.

2. The documents of the Second Vatican Council, as well as other church teaching

Commenting on these passages, the late Joseph A. Fitzmyer, SJ, summarized well for those Protestants who might retain certain suspicions about the Catholic approach to Scripture: "It thus emphasizes the inseparability of scripture and tradition and avoids saying that there are any revealed truths transmitted solely by tradition."[3]

An aspect of Catholic tradition has recently been attractive to evangelicals. Those with a keen sense of social responsibility have shown increasing interest in the Catholic social tradition, especially as advanced by Popes John Paul II and Benedict XVI; yet, as evangelicals, they retained a suspicion of how Catholics value tradition in relation to scripture. Hence, these remarks will dwell somewhat at length on the relationship between Scripture and tradition. Furthermore, since that presentation and discussion six years ago, the bishops of the United States have issued two more versions of *Forming Consciences for Faithful Citizenship* and Pope Francis has been elected. These remarks, therefore, involve considerable updating especially with regard to the 2015 version of the bishops' document.

HISTORY OF POLITICAL
RESPONSIBILITY/FAITHFUL CITIZENSHIP

The first year that the US bishops issued a statement on political responsibility for an election year was 1976.[4] That first version contained an important disclaimer: "We specifically do not seek the formation of a religious voting bloc; nor do we wish to instruct persons on how they should vote by endorsing candidates." That 1976 statement, which bore the title "Political Responsibility," forthrightly declared its purpose: "Without reference to political candidates, parties or platforms, we wish to offer a listing of some issues which we believe are central to the national debate this year." While the 1976 statement originated in the perceived need to present a consensus

---

documents, are cited by paragraph number. The Latin text of a promulgated document of the Second Vatican Council or Vatican II is the original text. This translation is from *Decrees of the Ecumenical Councils*, Volume Two, Trent to Vatican II, edited by Norman P. Tanner, SJ (Washington, DC: Georgetown University Press, 1990), 974–75.

3. Joseph A. Fitzmyer, SJ, "The Second Vatican Council and the Role of the Bible in Catholic Life," in *Faith, Word and Culture*, edited by Liam Bergin (Dublin: The Columba Press, 2004), 38.

4. "Political Responsibility, Statement of the U. S. Catholic Conference Administrative Board," *Origins: Catholic News Service Documentary Service*, vol. 5, issue 36 (February 26, 1976).

statement by US Catholic bishops, despite how the words or gestures of particular bishops were construed during the political campaign that year, by the most recent version in 2015, the statement offers more pointed advice. For example, note paragraph 35 in the 2015 version:

> There may be times when a Catholic who rejects a candidate's unacceptable position even on policies promoting an intrinsically evil act may reasonably decide to vote for that candidate for other morally grave reasons. Voting in this way would be permissible only for truly grave moral reasons, not to advance narrow interests or partisan preferences or to ignore a fundamental moral evil.

Strictly speaking, in the thirty-nine–year history of these statements, there was never a stated intention to create a voter's guide. Rather than telling Catholics how to vote, the succession of statements tried to focus on the common good and encourage Catholics to draw upon their consciences and to exercise prudence when voting. As the years and versions developed, the effort to avoid telling Catholics how to vote has come very close to telling Catholics how not to vote. Paragraph 34 of the 2011 version included the assertion that "a Catholic voter cannot vote for a candidate who takes a position in favor of an intrinsic evil, such as abortion or racism, if the voter's intent is to support that position." The sentence was expanded by adding more examples in 2015: "A Catholic cannot vote for a candidate who favors a policy promoting an intrinsically evil act, such as abortion, euthanasia, assisted suicide, deliberately subjecting workers or the poor to subhuman living conditions, redefining marriage in ways that violate its essential meaning, or racist behavior, if the voter's intent is to support that position." The 2015 version also retained an important sentence concluding that paragraph that advised avoiding single-issue voting: "At the same time, a voter should not use a candidate's opposition to an intrinsic evil to justify indifference or inattentiveness to other important moral issues involving human life and dignity."

In 1976, just three years after the Supreme Court decision on *Roe v. Wade* and with a pastoral plan for pro-life activities already approved and published by the bishops' conference, the leadership among US Catholic bishops was seriously concerned that some would exploit reactions to the Supreme Court decision on abortion to make the election mostly about this single issue when considering the qualifications of candidates for national office. In May 1976, US Catholic bishops, during their semi-annual meeting, endorsed *Political Responsibility*, which had been prepared by bishops' conference staff and adopted by the bishops' Administrative Committee in February. The committee's endorsement drew attention to the statement's call for "thoughtful and lively debate" on the issues, in the plural, that our country faced at that time and "a broad range of issues central to that debate." [5] Even so, there were occasions in 1976 and later in 1984, when bishops seemed to cross the line in identifying candidates who were not acceptable based on church teachings with regard to abortion.[6]

An obvious change over the years between the first document in 1976 and the most recent in 2015 is the expansion of specific issues. In 1976, the bishops agreed to nine public issues and listed them alphabetically: abortion, the economy, education, food policy, housing, human rights and US foreign policy, mass media, and military expenditures. The statement ran about five pages in thirty-one numbered paragraphs, and with fourteen notes at the end. There were some references to church documents and a few references to Scripture placed parenthetically in the text. The list of issues in 2015 expanded to thirteen and were not arranged alphabetically: human life; promoting peace; marriage and family life; religious freedom; preferential option for the poor and economic justice; health care; migration; Catholic education; promoting justice and countering violence; combatting unjust discrimination; care for our common home; communications, media, and culture; and global solidarity. While nothing is said specifically about why the issues are listed this way, this sentence in the paragraph preceding the listing suggests the listing is a prioritization of issues: "As the descriptions below indicate, some issues involve principles that can never be abandoned, such as the fundamental right to life and marriage as the union of one man and one woman." In actuality, one can argue that all thirteen issues rest on gospel principles. One can conclude this from two passages cited in the 2015 text, "all the earthly activities of the faithful will be bathed in the light of the Gospel" (a passage cited after paragraph 12 from the Second Vatican Council's *Pastoral Constitution in the Modern World,* "*Gaudium et Spes,*" 43) and "Its [the Church's] main aim is to interpret these [complex realities of life] realities, determining their conformity with or divergence from the lines of the Gospel teaching on man and his vocation, a vocation which is at once earthly and transcendent;

5. "U. S. Bishops' Resolution on Political Responsibility," *Origins,* vol. 6, issue 1 (May 27, 1976).

6. Timothy A. Byrnes provides examples for the 1976 and 1984 election years in his excellent study, *Catholic Bishops in American Politics* (Princeton, NJ: Princeton University Press, 1991), 74–81; 119–21.

its aim is thus to guide Christian behavior" (a passage cited in paragraph 60 from Pope John Paul II's 1987 encyclical *Sollicitudo Rei Socialis*, "The Social Concern of the Church," no. 41).

The 2015 statement runs considerably longer than the 1976 text which was five pages long with fourteen notes. The 2015 text is forty-two pages long with only eight notes but followed by a list of fourteen church documents cited parenthetically throughout the text. By contrast to earlier versions, in 2015 there is only one stand-alone citation to Scripture, John 13:34, "love one another." In the additional listing of documents in 2015, the titles fall under these categories: protecting human life, promoting family life, pursuing social justice, and practicing global solidarity, in that order, which might also be a prioritization of issues. Then, there is a listing of major speeches of Pope Francis during his September 2015 apostolic visit to the United States. There are numerous references to Pope Francis in the 2015 text.

Thus the text draws primarily from magisterial teaching. The magisterium or teaching office of the church is a major element of tradition, joined inseparably to Scripture and forming a single deposit of the word of God. Over its near forty-year history in the wake of the Second Vatican Council and its attempt to restore Scripture to the everyday life of Catholics, this teaching document on faithful citizenship has relied less and less on Scripture and has become a resounding reiteration of papal and other magisterial statements mostly on life issues. *Faithful Citizenship* is now a hefty booklet of almost fifty pages requiring attentive reading for several hours.[7]

THE ROLE OF THE CHURCH AND THE CATHOLIC VOTER

The underlying rationale for *Forming Consciences* is that the church "must not replace the state" but "must not remain on the sidelines in the fight for justice." This is language taken from the first encyclical of Pope Benedict XVI, *Deus Caritas Est*. The passage is quoted at length in *Forming Consciences*, paragraph 15.[8]

7. On the history of the text intention, see John Carr, "Faithful Citizenship: History, Context, Directions, Dangers," in *Faithful Citizenship: Principles and Strategies to Serve the Common Good*, edited by Dennis Hamm, SJ, and Gail S. Risch, *Journal of Religion & Society*, Supplement Series 4, The Kripke Center, Creighton University, 2008.

8. *Deus Caritas Est* bears the date of December 25, 2005, a little over eight months after the election of Benedict XVI. The passage that provides a basis for the rationale for *Forming Consciences* is paragraph 28: "The Church wishes to help form consciences in

More specifically, *Forming Consciences* provides a principle regarding what is morally evil that leaves politicians and voters, especially Catholic politicians and voters, very little room for maneuvering: "Those who knowingly, willingly, and directly support public policies or legislation that undermine fundamental moral principles cooperate with evil" (Paragraph 31). In ten places, the 2015 text refers to "intrinsically evil" acts beyond the already cited reference to a candidate's opposition to an "intrinsic evil" to justify the candidate's indifference to other social questions. For some readers, the concepts of intrinsic evil or cooperation with evil might pose problems. The text identifies "'intrinsically evil' actions" as "always incompatible with the love of God and neighbor," which are unquestionably the core messages of revelation, and thus are "always opposed to the authentic good of persons." Some Catholic ethicists have had difficulty with an exact meaning of intrinsic evil though they would allow, to some extent, actions to be qualified as "intrinsically evil." Adultery is never right, an example used by the *Catechism of the Catholic Church*, but the indices of both the *Catechism* and the *Compendium of the Social Doctrine of the Church*, another major listing of Catholic teaching, do not list "intrinsic evil." *Catechism* 1756 states what must be the closest definition of intrinsically evil acts without using the expression: "There are acts which, in and of themselves, independently of circumstances and intentions, are always gravely illicit by reason of their object; such as blasphemy and perjury, murder and adultery." The next brief sentence in the passage from the *Catechism* may or may not follow depending on what one includes under gravely illicit acts: "One may not do evil so that good may result from it." War, for example, is an evil, and John Paul II seemed to allow few exceptions. He certainly did not approve of the first and second US wars with Saddam Hussein's Iraq.

Forming Consciences states that the truths about human dignity and the sacredness of every human life are not only found in Scripture but "also come to us through the gift of human reason" (Paragraph 10). It is a teaching with a long history in the Catholic tradition that faith and reason can identify actions so evil that they "must always be rejected and opposed and must never be supported or condoned" (Paragraph 22). These assaults on

---

political life and to stimulate greater insight into the authentic requirements of justice as well as greater readiness to act accordingly, even when this might involve conflict with situations of personal interest. . . . The Church cannot and must not take upon herself the political battle to bring about the most just society possible. She cannot and must not replace the State. Yet at the same time she cannot and must not remain on the sidelines in the fight for justice."

human dignity include: abortion, euthanasia, human cloning, destructive research on human embryos, genocide, torture, racism, and targeting of noncombatants (Paragraphs 22–23). Acts of racism and the use of torture appear in another listing of "other unjust discrimination," including the use of the death penalty, resorting to unjust war, war crimes, failure to respond to those who are suffering from hunger or lack of health care, or an unjust immigration policy.

These moral concerns are said to be "not optional." The first listing is put forcefully to avoid the temptation of moral equivalence, making "no ethical distinction between different kinds of issues involving human life and dignity." The second listing is given to avoid a second temptation, the misuse of moral distinctions as a way of dismissing or ignoring other serious threats to human life and dignity (Paragraphs 28–29). Careful readers can discern the attempt within *Forming Consciences* to walk a thin line between exercising freedom to state church teaching with regard to public issues, and thus appealing to reason, and directing the faithful on how to vote.

Nowadays, with so much resentment towards congress and the presidency as institutions, the text's message is a radical one when it urges upon Catholics the necessity to be good citizens and the obligation to take an active part in public life as far as is possible in order to promote the common good. Important paragraphs of the *Catechism of the Catholic Church* (1913–1915) are quoted in paragraph 13 to support these reminders. The *Catechism* on this point refers to a passage in the *Pastoral Constitution on the Church in the Modern World*, "*Gaudium et Spes*" (31), when the bishops at the Second Vatican Council in 1965 praised those nations that provide a climate of genuine freedom to participate in public life.

THE TEXT ITSELF

One could write an assessment of the philosophical, theological, and methodological underpinnings of *Forming Consciences* by simply examining the text's handful of notes. Torture receives two of those precious eight notes, which are actually the same note given twice (notes 4 and 6) to the *Catechism of the Catholic Church*. That amounts to double emphases on torture, which "can never be justified." The reference is to a passage in the *Catechism* (2297) that defines torture and declares it contrary to respect for the person and for human dignity. That paragraph is followed in the *Catechism* (2298) by a paragraph length statement of regret that in times past these cruel practices were common and "often without protest from the Pastors of the Church" but that in recent times were neither necessary for public order nor in conformity with the legitimate rights of the human person. These references appeared in *Forming Consciences* for the 2008 national election when torture was very much on the minds of American citizens in light of revelations of White House memos instructing interrogators to use torture against suspected terrorists; these notes are truly extraordinary.[9]

The other six notes reference the following topics: the common good, the sources of erroneous judgment, direct and intentional destruction of innocent human life from the moment of conception until natural death that must always be opposed, the four major principles of Catholic social teaching (the dignity of the human person, subsidiarity, the common good and solidarity), the preventive use of military force, and a definition of marriage.

A distinguishing feature of the 2015 text is the increased number of references to redefinitions of marriage or the attempt to legitimize civil unions of same-sex couples as marriages. In fact, there seem to be more references to issues of defining marriage than even to abortion, economic justice, immigration, and religious persecution. In what seems a misplaced emphasis, paragraph 23 on racism and other social evils as mistreatment of workers and the poor are likened to "redefining marriage to deny its essential meaning."

Another distinguishing feature of the most recent version in 2015 is the inclusion of a number of references to the writings and speeches of Pope Francis, especially his apostolic journey to the United States in September 2015, less than two months before the final approval of the 2015 *Forming Consciences for Faithful Citizenship*. At least one purpose of the listing is an expression of support for Pope Francis. The text references Pope Francis's view of an "integral ecology" expounded in his 2015 encyclical, *Laudato Si'*. In all, there are about twenty references to actual statements by the current pope though he might have been cited even more times in references to major social issues around immigration, poverty and social and economic inequality, which are areas of his special pastoral concerns.

---

9. In 2006, the President of the USCCB, Bishop William Skylstad, signed a statement rejecting the use of torture. See: http://nccbuscc.org/comm/archives/2006/06-215.shtml (accessed 10/10/11). In June 2008, the USCCB issued "Torture is a Moral Issue: A Catholic Study Guide."

THEOLOGICAL PREMISES

What are the theological premises for the Catholic social teaching found in this text? Catholics believe that the Bible holds a privileged position as the normative source of Christian teaching and beliefs. Pope Benedict XVI called the Bible "the church's book."[10] The conciliar *Dogmatic Constitution on Divine Revelation (Dei Verbum)* has already been cited with regard to "a close connection and communication between sacred tradition and sacred scripture." That same passage continues with regard to tradition:

> For Sacred Scripture is the word of God inasmuch as it is con-
> signed to writing under the inspiration of the divine Spirit, while
> sacred tradition takes the word of God entrusted by Christ the
> Lord and the Holy Spirit to the Apostles, and hands it on to their
> successors in its full purity, so that led by the light of the Spirit of
> truth, they may in proclaiming it preserve this word of God faith-
> fully, explain it, and make it more widely known. (9)[11]

The bishops who gathered at Vatican II rejected a draft prepared by the Roman curia for the first period of the council in 1962 that over-emphasized scripture and tradition as two sources of revelation.[12] A commission, constituted according to the Council's procedures and approved by the assembly of bishops, jointly composed of members of the Council's Commission on the Doctrine of the Faith and Morals and the Secretariat for Promoting Christian Unity, prepared a new draft, which the Council eventually promulgated in 1965 during its final weeks. That document, *Dei Verbum*, was truly an act of the conciliar process of collegiality that characterized much of Vatican II.

The primary reference in *Dei Verbum* is to the Word of God, who is God incarnate in Christ. *Dei Verbum* defines Sacred Scripture as "the word of God inasmuch as it is consigned to writing under the inspiration of the

---

10. Post-Synodal Apostolic Exhortation, *Verbum Domini,* concluding the 2008 synod of bishops, "The Word of God in the Life and Mission of the Church." http://www.vatican.va/holy_father/benedict_xvi/apost_exhortations/documents/ hf_ben-xvi_exh_20100930_verbum-domini_en.html.

11. The document can be found on the Vatican website for the Second Vatican Council: http://www.vatican.va/archive/hist_councils/ii_vatican_council/documents/ vat-ii_const_19651118_dei-verbum_en.html .

12. See for example, John W. O'Malley, *What Happened at Vatican II* (Cambridge, MA: Harvard University Press, 2008), 141–52, which gives the history of these important developments.

divine Spirit" and tradition as transmitting "the word of God entrusted by Christ the Lord and the Holy Spirit to the Apostles, and hands it on to their successors in its full purity." Tradition surrounds Scripture. Tradition is how Scripture is interpreted and lived. Christ the Lord, in whom the entire revelation is summed up (2 Cor 1:20; 3:16—4:6), commanded apostles to preach the gospel, and the apostles and those whom they instructed handed on the preached Word by spoken word, by example, by what they instituted, and by writing down, under the inspiration of the Holy Spirit, the message of the salvific plan of God.[13]

In confidence that God will not abandon his church and that infallibility, inerrancy in teaching, belongs to the church on faith and morals, Catholics believe that when the representatives of their local churches, the bishops, gather universally in council, as last happened at the Second Vatican Council that produced *The Dogmatic Constitution on Divine Revelation*, and they declare together a specific teaching, supreme authority is exercised in the church. This is so for some of the statements in the sixteen documents of Vatican II, especially those following words such as, "this sacred synod declares" or "this sacred synod encourages." Such a passage appears in *Dei Verbum* (25): "The sacred synod also earnestly and especially urges all the Christian faithful, especially Religious, to learn by frequent reading of the divine Scriptures the 'excellent knowledge of Jesus Christ' (Phil 3:8)."

Evangelicals refer to biblical inerrancy. For Catholics, inerrancy applies to inspired teachings on salvation. To quote Joseph Fitzmyer again in reference to *Dei Verbum*, paragraph 11:

> When one comes to inerrancy, it has to be understood as a consequence of inspiration, but one that is not coterminous with it. It is restricted to inspired statements in the bible, and not to its questions, exclamations, or prayers. For the Constitution plainly states, "Since everything asserted by the inspired authors or sacred writers should be regarded as asserted by the Holy Spirit, it follows that we must acknowledge the books of scripture as teaching firmly, faithfully, and without error the truth that God wished to be recorded in the sacred writings for the sake of our salvation (11)."[14]

---

13. See *The Dogmatic Constitution on Revelation*, 7.

14. Fitzmyer, "The Second Vatican Council and the Role of the Bible in Catholic Life," 40. Fitzmyer cites the translation in Dean P. Bécherd, *The Scripture Documents: An Anthology of Official Catholic Teachings* (Collegeville, MN: Liturgical, 2002), 5.

Fr. Fitzmyer draws attention through the use of "asserted," used twice in the citation and "recorded," used once and concludes, "In other words, inerrancy is the quality of all assertions in the bible that pertain to human salvation."

As the Christians divided between east and west and further through the Reformation, the Catholic Church retained the belief that the one church of Christ can be found in the Catholic Church, though elements of truth and sanctification exist outside its visible boundaries.[15] Therefore, through its universal councils, which Paul VI also identified as general councils of the west subsequent to the division between the church east and west in the eleventh century, the church demonstrates its supreme authority that can be exercised if the bishops so choose and through the bishop of Rome, the pope, in communion with the bishops of the church. Other forms of conciliar counsel, for example through the actions of bishops' conferences, demonstrate the church's teaching authority. Obviously, an act of a universal council, like Vatican II, carries the greater authority than an act of an episcopal conference, but care is taken by bishops speaking pastorally as bishops or in conference to reflect conciliar teaching.

The *Pastoral Constitution on the Church in the Modern World (Gaudium et Spes)* is relevant to any discussion of *Forming Consciences*, not only because the conciliar document identifies among the many wrongs that poison human society "homicide, genocide, abortion, euthanasia" and "whatever violates the integrity of the human person," (27) but also because it opens with a call for a consistent ethic: "the joys and hopes, and sorrows and anxieties of people today, especially of those who are poor and afflicted, are also the joys and hopes, and sorrows and anxieties of the disciples of Christ."(1) *Gaudium et Spes* identifies "abortion and infanticide" as "abominable crimes."(51)[16]

Bishops gather in general council, which is presided over by the Bishop of Rome who has preeminence in authority in the western church and, Catholics believe, over the whole church. Catholic teaching on the role of the papacy became more pronounced in the second millennium, as the severance between the Church east and west became fixed. Papal documents, therefore, carry a special weight after conciliar texts for Catholics.

15. Second Vatican Council, *Dogmatic Constitution on the Church* (*Lumen Gentium*), 8.

16. An English translation of *Gaudium et Spes* can be found in Tanner, *The Decrees of the Ecumenical Councils*, Volume Two, Trent to Vatican II, 1069–1135.

Beginning in the late eighteenth century, popes revived the practice of circular letters or "encyclicals," and Pope Leo XIII, at the transition from nineteenth to the twentieth century and from agrarian society in Europe to industrial society, used this device of encyclical letters to address the pastoral concerns of the times. Leo XIII's *Rerum Novarum* on the rights of labor and the working poor is often designated the starting point of the modern Catholic social tradition.[17]

There are other papal documents besides encyclicals, for example, apostolic letters, apostolic exhortations, and apostolic constitutions. Papal addresses and speeches also carry a certain amount of weight, particularly if they broach a new topic or bring a strong emphasis to a topic that has moral currency, as Pius XI's comment in 1939 that we Christians are all spiritually Semites.[18]

Among important church teaching documents are the statements of conferences of bishops and of individual bishops. *Forming Conscience*, for example, cites the US bishops' *Living the Gospel of Life* (1998) in several places. Twice paragraph 5 of *Living the Gospel of Life* is cited in *Forming Consciences* with regard to abortion and euthanasia becoming preeminent threats to human life and dignity in American society (Paragraphs 22 and 64). *Forming Consciences* itself is an example of this collegial exercise of authority in the Catholic Church, rooted in the conciliar model, and respecting the communion of the whole church. Pope Francis, in a change of direction from his immediate predecessors, Popes John Paul II and Benedict XVI, often references the documents of national and regional conferences of bishops and thus draws attention to the importance of regional collegiality with regard to Catholic teaching.

No lasting success with regard to a teaching document of a bishops' conference comes without considerable effort to achieve consensus. A conference of bishops does not have the juridical authority to intervene in a diocese; yet, the more a consensus is achieved, the more persuasive bishops can be with one another. Paragraph 8 of *Forming Consciences* attempts to describe this delicate set of relations:

17. The declaration on papal infallibility of Vatican I in 1870 is not referenced here. Catholic scholars generally agree that this form of infallibility has been exercised only once subsequently. For the actual reference, see Tanner, "First Dogmatic Constitution on the Church of Christ," *Decrees of the Ecumenical Councils*, Volume II, 816.

18. Pius XI, "A Propos de L'Antisémitisme. Pèlerinage de la Radio catholique belge," *La Documentation Catholique* 39 (September 15, 1938), 1460–62.

During election years, there may be many handouts and voter guides that are produced and distributed. We encourage Catholics to seek those resources authorized by their own bishops, their state Catholic conferences, and the United States Conference of Catholic Bishops. This statement is intended to reflect and complement, not substitute for, the ongoing teaching of bishops in our own dioceses and states.

In 2007 and 2011, this paragraph concluded with a sentence following these words and serving as the final sentence: "In light of these reflections and those of local bishops, we encourage Catholics through the United States to be active in the political process, particularly in these challenging times." In 2015, a lengthy insertion was added after the above cited paragraph and the concluding sentence was retained. Here is the lengthy insertion:

When using this document, it is important to remember that Church teaching is coherent and rests on a comprehensive vision of the dignity of the human person, a dignity that St. John Paul II described as "manifested in all its radiance when the person's origin and destiny are considered: created by God in his image and likeness as well as redeemed by the most precious blood of Christ, the person is called a 'child in the Son' and a living temple of the Spirit, destined for the eternal life of blessed communion with God'" (*Christifideles Laici*, no. 37). Thus the particular judgements of the document may fall at various points along the political spectrum, but the foundational principles that guide these teachings should not be ignored in any case nor used selectively in order to serve partisan interests.[19]

What does a Catholic do when she or he disagrees with their bishop and even feels that the bishop is wrong? As a group, the bishops say this about *Forming Consciences*: "The judgments and recommendations that we make as bishops on specific issues do not carry the same moral authority as statements of universal moral teachings" (33). Thus, disagreement should not be on the principles themselves but on how they may be stated or applied. Nothing more is said in *Forming Consciences* pertinent to this point. Responsible Catholics are left to decide what to do, drawing from what is available to them.[20]

19. *Forming Consciences for Faithful Citizenship*, Paragraph 8, pages 11–12.

20. There is another element to the understanding of church authority, which has not been taken up because of space and focus, and that is the consent of the faithful, which Vatican II reiterated in its discussion of the prophetic role of Christ as exercised

PREMISES

Forming Consciences refers to human reason and expresses a confidence that reason also reaches many of the same truths of the faith based on human dignity (10). Reason is also served by faith: "We bring a consistent moral framework—drawn from basic human reason that is illuminated by Scripture and the teaching of the Church—for assessing issues, political platforms, and campaigns" (12). Catholics make moral judgments based on reason, drawing from the tenets of the faith and the whole of human sciences. Science ultimately poses no threat to the faith. In 1965, the bishops at Vatican II extolled the achievements of reason and the sciences, correctly understood to have limits.[21]

Pervading the acts of Vatican II and greatly influencing Giovanni Battista Montini, elected Pope Paul VI in June 1963 to guide the council to a successful conclusion, was the philosophical orientation often identified as personalism. Associated with the philosopher Emmanuel Mounier and developed within a renewed framework of the philosophy of thirteenth-century St. Thomas Aquinas in the first half of the twentieth century by Jacques Maritain, personalism provided a philosophically positive attitude towards the human person defined in and for relationships.[22] Montini read the French intellectual tradition, and his first encyclical as Paul VI, which was on the church, *Ecclesiam Suam*, introduced the concept of dialogue into the language of the Second Vatican Council and into Catholic tradition. The encyclical was issued halfway through the council and, though not an official "document of the council," could be understood as an act of the council because its content related so significantly to the content of major documents of Vatican II. The concept of dialogue cannot be found in previous conciliar documents. Dialogue is a core concept within a personalist framework. In addition, the concepts of human dignity and the preferential option for the poor rest on both a gospel foundation and a personalist understanding of human society. *Forming Consciences* cannot

---

by the church as the holy people of God and universal body of the faithful. See *Dogmatic Constitution on the Church (Lumen Gentium)*, 12.

21. See for example, *The Pastoral Constitution on the Church in the Modern World*, 5, 15, and 19.

22. Thomism, or the orientation in scholastic philosophy based on the writings of Thomas Aquinas, dominated Catholic seminary education for centuries leading up to Vatican II. Personalism arose partially as a badly needed renewal of Thomism and represented one of several new orientations flowing into the council.

be fully appreciated apart from understanding the personalist character of the acts of Vatican II and the way that the Church has implemented the council.[23]

Furthermore, *Forming Consciences* makes reference to "a consistent moral framework—drawn from basic human reason that is illuminated by Scripture and the teaching of the Church" (Paragraph 12) and how a consistent ethic of life provides a moral framework for principled Catholic engagement in political life and, rightly understood, neither treats all issues as morally equivalent nor reduces Catholic teaching to one or two issues (Paragraph 40). In past versions, for example in 2007 and 2011, this consistent moral framework was illustrated through seven key themes woven into this consistent ethic under the question of "What does the church say about Catholic social teaching in the public square?" These were: 1) the right to life and the dignity of the human person; 2) call to family, and participation, 3) community rights and responsibilities; 4) option for the poor and vulnerable; 5) dignity of work and the rights of workers; 6) solidarity; and 7) caring for God's creation (Paragraphs 40–54, 2011 version).

In 2015, these seven themes are replaced by four principles from the *Compendium of the Social Doctrine of the Church*: the dignity of the human person, subsidiarity, the common good, and solidarity. Reduction to these four principles leaves out specific reference to the poor and vulnerable and workers who together have been subjects of pastoral concern since Pope Leo XIII and to the current immigration crisis and the recent emphasis of caring for God's creation, and other pressing pastoral concerns expressed by Pope Francis. These are reduced to secondary themes, which are not even subheadings. Thus, though the 2015 text is lengthier and more verbose than previous versions, it has less specificity on a wider range of social issues.

Finally, one could overlook another philosophical premise because it seems commonplace to us as we think about the strengths of our nation, namely, the religious pluralism guaranteed by the Bill of Rights. In paragraph 11, *Forming Consciences* states that "Our nation's tradition of pluralism is enhanced, not threatened, when religious groups and people of faith bring their convictions and concerns into public life." A similar statement appeared in the 1976 *Political Responsibility*: "The church's participation in public affairs is not a threat to the political process or to genuine pluralism,

---

23. Cf. Cardinal Avery Dulles, SJ, *Dialogue, Truth, and Communion* (New York: National Pastoral Life Center for Catholic Common Ground Initiative, 2001), 2–3.

but an affirmation of their importance." *Forming Consciences* is essentially an American document in which the first person plural "we" is invoked as Catholic citizens of the American republic.

New to the 2015 text are several additions on religious freedom. One wonders if it is true that "the longstanding tax exemption of the Church has been explicitly called into question at the highest levels of government, precisely because of her teachings on marriage" (Paragraph 72). The teachings of Vatican II developed in the *Declaration on Religious Liberty* (*Dignitatis Humanae*) were a new development of explicit Catholic teaching in 1965. It was produced in a world that was divided by a cold war where religious rights were clearly suppressed in communist regimes. The Declaration was also produced in a world where religious pluralism was beginning to be appreciated by church leaders as an asset to democratic societies. That was a different time fifty years earlier from the 2015 and the latest version of *Forming Consciences*. The text notes two temptations in contemporary democracies when making political decisions: making no distinctions on moral issues and ignoring priorities. These are principles that people of faith can bring to public discussion with those whose faith may differ from their own and with those who would agree to reasonable discussion for the common good. The second temptation on prioritization might need more careful attention when compromising religious liberty appears in a list including racism, war crimes, and environmental degradation.

CONCLUDING THOUGHTS

Forming Consciences and its predecessors back to *Political Responsibility* in 1976 have existed for all but ten of the years that the US Conference of Catholic Bishops has existed.[24] The conference was formed during the working sessions of the Second Vatican Council in 1964 as an implementa-

---

24. A National Catholic Welfare Conference, a body of voluntary membership for Catholic bishops of the United States and with considerable moral authority, existed from the time of the First World War as an effort to coordinate Catholic responses to the war, especially the resulting refugee crisis. It issued pastoral statements during the years of its existence, prior to the emphasis on episcopal collegiality at Vatican II. In 1964, during the Second Vatican Council, the Catholic Bishops of the United States formed the National Conference of Catholic Bishops to include committees focused on the initiatives of the councils. The offices of the Welfare Conference became part of a sister organization, the US Catholic Conference. In 2001, the two were merged in the US Conference of Catholic Bishops.

tion of the *Dogmatic Constitution on the Church* (*Lumen Gentium*), promulgated in November of that year, and of its collegial vision of the exercise of episcopal authority. Episcopal conferences were formed to implement the initiatives of the Second Vatican Council. For most of that history from 1964 to 2017, there has been a statement on political responsibility.

One can see over the years of its development that current public issues influenced how the bishops chose to modify and expand the text to the present form. Whereas the initial text was a document of the conference's Administrative Committee, since a statement was needed while the 1976 campaign was unfolding, the more recent texts have increasingly involved several major committees of the conference. At times, considerable effort and dedication of time was needed by a drafting and review committee of bishops who labored over numerous suggestions from their fellow US bishops as well as more recent church documentation to make the text relevant to the current political climate of the United States. That was not an easy task and the outcome varied from version to version. The intention was to remind Catholics of important principles in forming their consciences and exercising prudence while participating in the political process as citizens.

PART TWO

Immigration, Racism, the Sanctity
of Human Life, and Peace

6

Immigration: A Survey of Biblical Teaching in Evangelical Perspective

M. Daniel Carroll R. (Rodas)

MY BRIEF FOR THIS essay is to offer an evangelical perspective on immigration.[1] This is a difficult task for at least two fundamental reasons. To begin with, evangelicalism is an incredibly diverse movement. Evangelicals do not speak with one mind, nor do we possess a universally accepted official voice on issues. A general consensus exists on some issues, but I am afraid that no such agreement exists on the topic at hand. A second reason, and this is related to the first, is that there is no historic or official tradition of social teaching or an ecclesial office to which evangelicals can appeal in order to ground their thinking on these matters. These realities can yield thinking that is fragmented and theologically thin. This has certainly been true in regards to immigration.

This is not the state of affairs for the Catholic Church.[2] In June 1988 John Paul II established The Pontifical Council for the Pastoral Care of Migrants and Itinerant People. This department of the Roman Curia produces valuable documents on topics related to world migration, such as the 2004

1. This essay limits its discussion to evangelicals in the United States.

2. For a helpful summary and discussion of Roman Catholic teaching on immigration, see Carmen Nanko-Fernández, "Roman Catholic: A 'Documented' Response: Papal Teaching and People on the Move," in *Immigrant Neighbors among Us: Immigration across Theological Traditions*, eds. M. D. Carroll R. and L. A. Sánchez M. (Eugene, OR: Wipf and Stock, 2015), 1–21.

Instruction *Erga Migrantes Caritas Christi* (*The Love of Christ towards Migrants*). Its website provides links to other materials, including papal messages delivered for the annual World Migration Day. Popes John Paul II and Benedict XVI argued for the care of the foreigner, and Francis has continued that charge. The Council's counterpart in this country is the United States Conference of Catholic Bishops' Committee on Migration. In 2003 the Bishops' Conferences of Mexico and the United States collaborated on *Strangers No Longer: Together on the Journey of Hope* and have released periodic documents supporting immigration reform. Scholarly interest in immigration and pastoral commitment to immigrants are evident in publications at various levels of academic discourse[3] and church-wide initiatives. There are parish initiatives, and many Catholic organizations are involved in helping immigrant communities in multiple ways. In other words, Roman Catholic attention to the issue is long-standing, deeply theological, pastoral, international, and local. There is much that evangelicals can learn.

The landscape among evangelicals, however, is changing. On the one hand, a growing number of denominations representing a broad sweep of doctrinal positions have made statements on immigration that look with favor and compassion on immigrants (see a list of websites in the appendix). The increasing prominence of the topic of immigration on the national scene and within its member denominations and organizations prompted the National Association of Evangelicals (NAE) to revisit its earlier statements (resolutions appeared in 1995 and 2006) to produce in 2009 a new and fuller resolution that calls for reforming present immigration policy.[4] Book-length studies have appeared.[5] Many denominations have

---

3. E.g., Jean-Pierre Ruiz, *Readings from the Edges: The Bible and People on the Move* (Maryknoll, NY: Orbis, 2011); Daniel G. Groody and Gioacchino Campese, eds., *A Promised Land, A Perilous Journey* (Notre Dame, IN: University of Notre Dame Press), 2008.

4. http://nae.net/immigration-2009/.

5. Mark R. Amstutz, *Just Immigration: American Policy in Christian Perspective* (Grand Rapids: Eerdmans, 2017); Joseph Castleberry, *The New Pilgrims: How Immigrants Are Renewing America's Faith and Values* (Franklin, TN: Worthy, 2015); M. Daniel Carroll R., *Christians at the Border: Immigration, the Church, and the Bible* (2nd ed.; Grand Rapids: Baker, 2013); Matthew Soerens and Jenny Hwang, *Welcoming the Stranger: Justice, Compassion & Truth in the Immigration Debate* (Downers Grove, IL: InterVarsity, 2009). In contrast, James K. Hoffmeier argues that biblical teaching applies only to legal immigrants in *The Immigration Crisis: Immigrants, Aliens, and the Bible* (Wheaton: Crossway, 2009). These works are designed to engage an informed lay audience. There are many publications of a more technical sort.

begun Hispanic ministries dedicated to church planting, and several are establishing training programs for lay and pastoral leadership. The growing awareness, here and abroad, of the potential contribution of immigrant communities to the worldwide mission of the Christian faith has generated what is called diaspora missiology.[6]

These publications and ministry efforts usually come from the perspective of the majority culture. Yet, there are millions of evangelical believers within the immigrant community and the thousands of Hispanic churches (whether immigrant or nonimmigrant).[7] The Hispanic evangelical subculture has its own particular ecclesiastical and theological characteristics and its own organizations, both those within majority culture denominational structures as well as those born outside these groups. The largest evangelical national organization is the National Hispanic Christian Leadership Conference (NHCLC). Other prominent organizations include Esperanza USA and the National Latino Evangelical Coalition (NaLEC). There are Hispanic evangelical publishing and recording companies (as divisions within existing evangelical companies or as independent efforts), as well as nationally known conference speakers, authors, and artists. Because of my bicultural background (I am half-Guatemalan), my experience has been with Hispanics, but it would be helpful to investigate similar realities among other immigrant communities, whether larger ones like the Koreans and Chinese or smaller groups. The relevant point for this discussion is to recognize that reflection on immigration issues by evangelical Christians of the majority culture should take into consideration that a large portion of the immigration population are brothers and sisters in Christ, not a faceless mass of foreigners.

The purpose of this essay is to survey some of the biblical and theological foundations for the immigration debate in the hope that it can help inform evangelicals and others as they grapple with this difficult issue. Both

6. Sadiri Joy Tira and Tetsunao Yamamori, eds., *Scattered and Gathered: A Global Compendium of Diaspora Missiology* (Oxford: Regnum, 2016); Enoch Wan, ed., *Diaspora Missiology: Theory, Methodology, and Practice* (Seattle: CreateSpace, 2012); Lausanne Committee for World Evangelization, *Scattered to Gather: Embracing the Global Trend of Diaspora* (Manila: LifeChange, 2010).

7. Note, e.g., Samuel Pagán, ed., *The Hispanic Evangelical Church: History, Ministry and Challenges* (Elk Grove, CA: NHCLC, 2016); Daniel A. Rodríguez, *A Future for the Latino Church: Models for Multilingual, Multigenerational Hispanic Congregations* (Downers Grove, IL: IVP Academic, 2012); Juan Francisco Martínez, *Los Protestantes: An Introduction to Latino Protestantism in the United States* (Santa Barbara, CA: Praeger, 2011).

evangelicals and Roman Catholics turn to the Scripture for guidance, and ideally this kind of study can provide additional grounding in the articulation of a genuinely Christian perspective on immigration.

Four preliminary observations are in order. First, there can be a gap between the more pro-immigrant perspectives and pastoral concerns of many evangelical leaders and denominational heads and those of the person in the pew. Many churchgoers are not well-informed about the many issues related to immigration, immigrant experiences, and biblical teaching related to immigration. Consequently, a percentage of evangelicals of the majority culture sometimes define their position more by their political party affiliation and its ideology and express their view with the impassioned rhetoric of some in the media. For example, there were both positive and negative responses among evangelicals to the compromise bipartisan Senate bill (of the "Gang of Eight") on immigration in June, 2013. More recently, some evangelicals either tolerated or embraced the anti-immigrant position of Donald Trump, the Republican candidate in the 2016 presidential election. Those in leadership are aware of this and move ahead cautiously. They are cognizant of the need to educate their constituencies, hoping to lead them forward in such a way so as not to lose their ear.

Second, these initial observations have concentrated on evangelicalism. Mainline denominations and groups are much more organized on this issue. For example, the National Council of Churches through their Justice and Advocacy Commission, along with several of their state offices and member communions, have made statements, published materials, and sponsored activities. Member denominations and affiliated scholars are publishing a variety of studies on the topic,[8] and some ecumenical church bodies coordinate their efforts with immigrant activist organizations.

Third, immigration is a topic that has generated cooperation across theological and ecclesial lines. In addition to efforts like Catholics and Evangelicals for the Common Good, Christian faith coalitions are speaking out and acting on the issue.[9] At the national level, for instance, World

8. E.g., Miguel A. De La Torre, *The U.S. Immigration Crisis: Toward an Ethics of Place* (Cascade Companions; Eugene, OR: Cascade, 2016); Ched Myers and Matthew Colwell, *Our God Is Undocumented: Biblical Faith and Immigrant Justice* (Maryknoll, NY: Orbis, 2012); Ben Daniel, *Neighbor: Christian Encounters with "Illegal" Immigration* (Louisville: Westminster John Knox, 2010).

9. An international compendium modeling this shared commitment at an academic level is vanThanh Nguyen and John M. Prior, eds., *God's People On the Move: Biblical and Global Perspectives on Migration and Mission* (Eugene, OR: Pickwick, 2014).

Relief, the social outreach arm of the NAE, has helped organize conferences on immigration on several college campuses. This topic is bringing together Catholics, evangelicals, the mainline, and Jews.

Fourth, the following discussion is limited to the Bible and theology. A comprehensive presentation would include other items, such as the history of immigration (especially into this country), a survey of past and present US immigration law, the impact of immigration on economic, labor, health, and law enforcement issues, and consideration of current world migration issues (such as the flow of remittances, global labor movements and agreements, the international drug trade, and human trafficking).[10]

BIBLICAL AND THEOLOGICAL FOUNDATIONS

Evangelicals make the claim that theirs is a faith grounded in the revelation of God found in the Scripture. This next part of this paper, therefore, turns to the Bible for guidance on the issue of immigration. This is not to suggest in any way that other Christian traditions do not probe the Bible on this matter. Footnotes to previous pages in this essay confirm that fact. It is just that this direct appeal to the Bible in all matters of faith and practice is a peculiarly evangelical claim. Evangelical groups and churches especially desire to know what the Bible has to say about immigration before they hear other data and points of debate.

It is important to be aware that presentations on the Bible and immigration have two sets of listeners. There are those of the majority culture who must be made aware of the relevant biblical material; this is a ministry of *exposure* and *education*. On the other hand, there are the immigrant populations who find in this exposition something more: *encouragement* and *empowerment*.[11] This section offers an overview of what the Bible says from both perspectives.[12]

10. Mary C. Waters and Reed Ueda, eds., *The New Americans: A Guide to Immigration since 1965* (Cambridge, MA: Harvard University Press, 2007); Aristide R. Zohlberg, *A Nation by Design: Immigration Policy in the Fashioning of America* (New York: Russell Sage Foundation; Cambridge, MA: Harvard University Press, 2006); cf. Elena Fiddian-Qasmiyeh et al., eds., *The Oxford Handbook of Refugee & Forced Migration Studies* (Oxford: Oxford University Press, 2014).

11. M. Daniel Carroll R., "How to Shape Christian Perspectives on Immigration? Strategies for Communicating Biblical Teaching," in *Religion and Politics in America's Borderlands*, ed. S. Azaransky (Lanham, MD: Lexington, 2013), 57–77.

12. For more details, see Carroll R., *Christians at the Border*. Additional studies on

A Majority Culture Perspective

Image of God. The starting point of a biblical orientation to the topic of immigration will determine in large measure the tone and direction of the discussion. Not a few begin with Romans 13 and the idea of submitting to the government. This is applied in this debate to mean that legality is the fundamental and defining issue. Although it is important to deal with legal matters, is this the best place *to begin* the discussion?

Our proposal is that the best place to begin is with the image of God in Genesis 1 (vv. 26–28). Historically there have been differences of opinion as to what the image refers. Some hold to an ontological view—that is, the image of God concerns what humans are and what they possess. Usually this is considered to mean that humans have a will, intellect, emotions, and a spiritual component (this more Reformed position differs from Roman Catholic dogma, but both lean in this direction). Others argue for a relational perspective; this is the Lutheran view. Still others believe that the image is best understood functionally. That is, the image highlights humanity's unique capacity and responsibility to rule as God's vice-regents on earth.

All of these options agree that every person has supreme value and potential. Immigrants, too, are made in the image of God. Therefore, they have inherent worth and are worthy of respect. As creatures made in the image of God, they also have much to contribute. This foundational starting point moves the debate away from defining immigration fundamentally in terms of cultural identity, economic impact, national security, and legality. These all are topics that need to be dealt with at the appropriate time; it is just that they are not the place to start the conversation. Immigration, above all else, is about persons who are precious in the sight of God. A clear understanding of this theological point will orient in profound ways how the pragmatic questions are handled.

Old Testament Narratives. The human element of displaced people is abundantly evident in Old Testament narratives. One could go to the creation mandate to "fill the earth" (Gen 1:28). This spreading out over the planet requires movement. Perhaps it could be said that migration is part of what it means to be human. Indeed, the history of humanity is the history of migrations.

---

specific parts of the Old Testament are cited in the following footnotes.

More particularly, the story of the chosen people starts with Terah's move from Ur to Haran and from there to Canaan (Gen 11:31—12:5). It is a history that is generated by migration (cf. Deut 26:5). In these Old Testament accounts individuals and families move for any number of reasons. Sometimes this change is voluntary; in other cases, people are exiled as victims of forced removal after defeat in war or have fled armed conflict. While a technical distinction can be drawn between those migrating of their own volition and those who may be more precisely labeled exiles or refugees, the significant point for our purposes is the commonalities of experiences across these different categories of people now living outside their homeland.

Of those who leave of their own accord, several migrate to survive. In Genesis, the patriarchs Abraham, Isaac, and Jacob (and his sons and their families) travel to secure food (Egypt in Gen 12; 42–46; the Negev in Gen 20; Philistia in Gen 26). Naomi and her family leave Bethlehem and cross to the other side of the Dead Sea to Moab in a time of famine (Ruth 1:1). Years later, now widowed, Naomi moves back to her homeland with Ruth, her daughter-in-law. Naomi the immigrant has returned home, and now Ruth becomes an immigrant. Survival is still the issue for these two women, however, and so Ruth goes to the fields to glean from what is left by Boaz's harvesters.[13]

Other stories recount how others are forced from their homes. Jacob flees north to Aram from the wrath of his brother Esau and lives for a time under Laban's roof (Gen 27–31). Joseph is betrayed by his brothers and sold into slavery. He overcomes difficult circumstances, rises to become second to Pharaoh in Egypt, and helps save that nation from starvation. He is the one who paves the way for Jacob and those same brothers to migrate to the Nile Delta and settle in Goshen (Gen 27; 39–41; 46–47). Centuries later, thousands are taken into exile, when Israel falls to Assyria (eighth-century BCE) and Judah to Babylon (sixth-century BCE).

Life in other lands could be harsh. In time, the ruler of Egypt forgot Joseph's contributions, and the Israelites become slave labor for his building projects (Exod 1). Egyptian sources describe the measures, which that country took to keep out some of those seeking sustenance (e.g., establishing a series of forts east of the Nile River). Inscriptional evidence indicates that some of those in the Assyrian exile became domestic servants, while

---

13. Carroll R., "Once a Stranger, Always a Stranger? Immigration, Assimilation, and the Book of Ruth," *International Bulletin of Missionary Research* 39, no. 4 (2015) 185–88.

others were assigned to work on farms or in construction. Psalm 137 expresses the feelings of anger, shame, and homesickness of those removed from Judah by Babylon. Not everyone, though, endured such harsh fates. In Egypt some foreigners were taken in and became part of society at some level (like Joseph; or Moses, Exod 1–2). Daniel is deported to Babylon and lives in the royal precincts, where he serves several kings with wisdom. Esther's uncle Mordecai seems to have been a man of some means, and this young woman becomes queen of the Persian Empire. Nehemiah is cupbearer to the Persian king Artaxerxes, while Ezra and Ezekiel minister among their people.

Old Testament Law. Immigration requires legislation. It has always been so. The law codes of Israel are testimony to the inescapable necessity of dealing with the wages of those from the outside, their legal standing and rights, and degrees of integration.[14]

As in most societies, sojourners in Israel were a vulnerable group (they are classified with the poor, widows, and orphans as those most at risk). In the ancient world, where there were no governmental assistance programs of the sort that we have today, people had to rely on extended family. The challenge for foreigners was that they were separated from the kinship networks that would have been able to help them in the trials of life. Another issue was that they were excluded from the land tenure system. Property was to stay within the family and be passed on through male heirs. This situation of outsiders was problematic in an agrarian peasant society like Israel: without family and land, they were at the mercy of the Israelites for work, provision, and protection. The impression that one gets from these realities is that foreigners often were day laborers.

People in these conditions can be taken advantage of. For outsiders, sustenance can be a constant challenge; they can be overworked and underpaid (or not paid at all); and they can find themselves defenseless and without recourse in legal dealings. Old Testament Law responded to this vulnerability with a series of measures. Foreigners qualified, along with those other needy groups, to glean at harvest time (Lev 19:10; Deut 24:19–22) and for the triennial tithe (Deut 14:28–29). They were to be given rest

---

14. Carroll R., "Welcoming the Stranger: Toward a Theology of Immigration in Deuteronomy," in *For Our Good Always: Studies on the Message and Influence of Deuteronomy in Honor of Daniel I. Block*, ed. J. S. DeRouchie, J. Gile, and K. J. Turner (Winona Lake, IN: Eisenbrauns, 2013), 441–62.

on the Sabbath (Exod 20:10; Deut 5:14) and to be paid a fair wage on time (Deut 24:14–15). No one was to take advantage of them in the courts (Deut 1:16–17; 27:19).[15]

Why obey these laws? What motivation would Israelites have to treat outsiders so compassionately? The Torah gives two primary reasons. First, Israel is to remember that it had been born as a people made up of despised foreigners, workers in Egypt's oppressive system, who by the grace of God had been redeemed. They came from immigrant stock, so they were to be benevolent to the foreigners in their midst. They were never to forget their history. That history defined them, and their treatment of the outsider was a measure of their faith in God (Lev 19:18; 33–34; Exod 23:9). To forget would result in their doing similar things to what the Egyptians had done so many years before. The Israelites, in fact, would always be "strangers" in the land of which God was owner and patron (Lev 25:23). Second, and more importantly, they were to love the sojourner because God does. True faith was inseparable from charity toward the disadvantaged, among whom were numbered the sojourners (Deut 10:14–19; cf. Ps 146:9; Jer 7:4–8; Zech 7:8–10; Mal 3:5). These are moral, theological, and missional appeals, driven not by rules of strict exclusion but rather by a gracious concern for the needy.

Even though these laws were for Israel—its time, place, culture, and faith—their significance was and is more far-reaching. Deuteronomy 4:5–8 states that these laws were to be a witness to the other nations of the character of God. These laws, in the particular model of society that was ancient Israel, in some way reflected the heart of God. Other nations might have their own laws with their own cultural and socioeconomic configurations, but these divine values would remain, transcending the boundaries of his people.

The New Testament. An examination of the New Testament material begins with Jesus. Jesus and his family flee to Egypt when he was a small child to escape Herod's rampage (Matt 2). Although we have no information about their sojourn there (place or length of stay), they perhaps became part of the large Jewish community in Egypt. Whatever the case, Jesus was

---

15. After the exile there was the fear that foreigners could lead Israel away from faith in God and adversely affect the social life of the community through intermarriage (Ezra 9–10; Nehemiah 13:23–28; cf. 1 Kings 11:3–8). This was a reaction linked to that unique situation, the discussion of which goes beyond the scope of this essay.

a refugee for a time in a foreign land. Life in another place was part of his personal experience.

In his teaching Jesus never dealt directly with the topic of immigration. Nevertheless, two items are relevant. To begin with, Jesus involved himself with those who were different and despised. On several occasions he lifted up the Samaritans, a loathsome people to many Jews. Jesus spoke with a Samaritan woman at the well in John 4, and in Luke 10 he uses a Samaritan as a paragon of righteousness in his response to the question "Who is my neighbor?" The neighbor whom the expert in the law was to love was the loathed Samaritan. This teaching is consistent with his call to reach out to the marginalized, such as women, the poor, and the sick. The other item that many point to is Jesus' pronouncement in Matthew 25 about caring for the stranger (vv. 35, 38, 43–44). This is a powerful assertion, but the referent is disputed. It is possible that "the least of these" (vv. 40, 45) refers to disciples (cf. Matt 10:42; 18:6, 10, 14); if that were the case, these would be disciples who would suffer for his sake (cf. 1 Cor 16:5–9; Gal 4:13–14; 3 John 5–10). This passage, however, continues to be utilized by many in discussions on immigration.

The New Testament epistles also are relevant. They reveal that the citizenship of Christians ultimately lies elsewhere (Phil 3:20; Heb 13:14). Therefore, national and ethnic loyalties cannot take priority over kingdom demands. In addition, hospitality towards others, whether fellow believers or unfamiliar persons, is a Christian virtue. All Christians are to be gracious to others (Rom 12:13; Heb 13:2; 1 Pet 4:9). This quality is to characterize especially the leadership of the church (1 Tim 3:2; Titus 1:8). First Peter speaks of believers as "aliens and strangers" (1:1; 2:11). Interestingly, the addressees of this letter may have been literal exiles. If so, that legal standing in the Roman Empire reflected and deepened their spiritual status as Christians. More importantly, these passages teach that migration is a central metaphor of what it means to be a Christian. Those who migrate often are defenseless and dependent, sensing the strangeness of their new surroundings—all apt descriptions of being followers of Christ in a world not our own.

Both testaments have much to instruct those of the majority culture in the United States. This brief survey of the biblical material shows that immigrants are worthy of respect, that migration is part of human experience, and that many biblical "heroes" were displaced persons. The Law underscores that legislation must be benevolent to the vulnerable. Israel's experience should serve as a reminder that this country's history is a tale of immigrants and that this memory should shape attitudes toward newcomers today. Jesus forces believers to consider the possibility that those who are different may be the very ones that can lead us to a deeper faith, while the epistles call us to care for the outsider. After all, every Christian is an outsider.

Immigrants and the Biblical Teaching

While there is much that a receiver/host, or majority, culture can glean from the Scripture, there also is much for immigrants.[16] Immigrants find assurance of their worth and comfort through the accounts of others in the narratives who had similar experiences. The Bible can empower them to live life in assurance of the grace of God and to seek constructive change in their situation with his help and that of others of like mind. Some items that could be mentioned include:

- The image of God. Every immigrant has worth and potential. There is no need to feel inferior or to live life as a second-class person. But the fact of the image also makes a claim on immigrants. It can serve as a motivation to develop skills for the common good and to live responsibly as God's representatives.

- Old Testament narratives. These accounts can serve a dual purpose. On the one hand, immigrants discover accounts of people in the Bible with which they can identify; at the same time, those lives serve as examples of how to live faithfully and to contribute to the host society (e.g., Joseph, Ruth, Ezra, Nehemiah, Daniel).

- The Law of Israel. The legislation related to sojourners was gracious and generous, but mutuality was assumed as well. Foreigners would have been expected to learn the laws (Deut 31:10–13) and observe many other regulations and customs of the land. Penalties for violations were to be the same for native and outsider alike (Lev 24:22;

---

16. M. Daniel Carroll R., "Reading the Bible through Other Lenses: New Vistas from an Hispanic Diaspora Perspective," in *Global Voices: Reading the Bible in the Majority World*, eds. C. S. Keener and M. D. Carroll R. (Peabody, MA: Hendrickson, 2012), 5–26; cf. Luis Rivera Rodríguez, "Toward a Diaspora Hermeneutics (Hispanic North America)," in *Character Ethics and the Old Testament: Moral Dimensions of Scripture*, eds. M. D. Carroll R. and J. Lapsley (Louisville: Westminster John Knox, 2007), 169–89.

Num 15:29). In sum, to live in another country requires respect for their ways of life.

- The example of Jesus and New Testament teaching. To follow Jesus is to respond to those who are unlike us, and this host country is no different! The strangeness is mutual, and in their weakness immigrant believers can reach out to majority culture Christians. All are fellow pilgrims, "strangers in a strange land"—although for the immigrant that strangeness is not only spiritual; it is also racial, cultural, social, political, and linguistic.

Another issue, which surfaces in the biblical texts, that is pertinent to both host culture and immigrant population, is integration into the host society. The Old Testament narratives that were mentioned earlier, as well as others, serve as object lessons of this accommodation or assimilation process.

- Expected or assumed assimilation: Israel was told by God to allow sojourners to participate in many of the religious feasts (e.g., Exod 20:8–11; 12:48–49; Lev 16:29–30; Deut 16:11, 14). This opened up the most precious part of the nation's identity to outsiders. To do this, sojourners may have been expected to convert to the faith of Israel (or at the very least respect it), be aware of proper procedures, and to know the language of the land (Hebrew).

- Little integration. Ezra, as a priest, does not seem to have assimilated very much to his Persian surroundings. His desire is to go back to the land of Israel and to reestablish life according to the demands of the Law. There were some in exile who felt humiliated, angry, and desperately longed for home (Ps 137).

- Significant integration. In a letter to those in exile, Jeremiah urges them to plan for a long stay and to invest their lives in their new home for the common good and for their own benefit. It was assumed that they would not forsake all of their culture or their faith in the God of Israel (Jer 29:1–7). Daniel and his friends are given a new name and an education in Babylonian matters to prepare them for service to the empire, but they maintain the dietary laws and openly testify of their faith. Daniel continues his practice of prayer even as he loyally works for the crown (Dan 1–6). Nehemiah is cupbearer to the king, but still is attentive to news from his ancestral land. He leaves with the king's permission and help in order to rebuild the walls of Jerusalem and revitalize the Jewish society as governor; after a time, he returns to his post in the Persian court.

- Almost total assimilation. Joseph accepts an Egyptian name, marries an Egyptian, and has two sons by her—yet he gives them Hebrew names (Gen 41:45, 50–52). His appearance is so Egyptian that his brothers do not recognize him, but interestingly, he had not forgotten his mother tongue; he understood when they spoke and then revealed himself to them. At the end of his life, though he would be embalmed according to Egyptian custom, he asks to be buried in his homeland (Gen 42–45, 50). Ruth leaves her native Moab and embarks on a journey to another land and people (Ruth 1:16–17), begins the process of integrating into Bethlehem, and finally is accepted into the community through her marriage to Boaz (ch. 4). Esther (she also has a Hebrew name, Hadassah, 2:7), a few generations removed from the fall of Jerusalem and the exile, is reminded by her kinsman Mordecai of her obligation to her people. Apparently he had done well financially and socially, and so he sits at the city gate with other community leaders (e.g., Esther 3:2; 5:9). That this prosperous foreigner refuses to do him homage infuriates Haman, yet Mordecai demonstrates his loyalty to the king by uncovering an assassination plot (2:21–23). Esther is able to save her people, but there is no indication that she or Mordecai ever contemplated returning to the land.

These cases exemplify different processes and degrees of cultural, linguistic, and sociopolitical integration. It is also interesting to track the varied responses of the host peoples—from Egyptian anxieties of being overrun by large numbers of foreign workers to the inclusion of Ruth by the Bethlehemites to the deep trust Artaxerxes has in Nehemiah and that Nebuchadnezzar and Darius have in Daniel. These reactions are accompanied by political decisions and social arrangements. In other words, the treatment of outsiders, however they arrived, was an issue in the ancient world even as it is today. The process of accommodation for both sides is complex and determined by many factors. These stories can encourage immigrants by demonstrating that their situation is not unique and that God is with them wherever they or the host culture find themselves on the spectrum of integration.

An Inadequate Proof-Text: Romans 13

It may be too much of a generalization to say that evangelicals often have tended to lean toward conservative politics. This statement is overly simplistic, and recent elections testify to the diversity of evangelical political persuasions. Still, many appeal to the "rule of law" in discussions on immigration. The conviction is that the United States historically has been a nation that respects the law and that evangelicals must be law-abiding citizens. In relationship to immigration, this perspective interprets the present current state of affairs as: undocumented immigrants have broken the law, are by definition illegal, and thus are deserving of the law's penalties (even deportation). The biblical basis for this position is Romans 13:1–7.

This stance deserves a response on several fronts, including clarification on the realities of the history of immigration and the development of immigration legislation in this country. The uninformed assumption of many is that this legal history matches the sentiments of the Statue of Liberty, that the folklore related to Ellis Island characterizes most immigrant experiences, and that the laws have been and are eminently fair. This is not the place to survey these matters, but any substantive knowledge of these areas yields the inescapable admission that this history and American immigration policies over the years have been complicated, contradictory, and not always equitable. These areas of research, though, are beyond the purview of this essay.

So, I return to the Bible. If evangelicals claim to shape their worldview by the Word of God, then it is imperative to place this passage within the broad scope of Scripture and not make this an isolated text for anti-immigrant sentiments. The Bible as a whole moves its readers in a very different direction than would this myopic and limited biblical argument that limits itself to Romans 13. To say this does not mean that current US law is of no importance or that the nation's borders are irrelevant. It is to say, though, that the best way to approach this topic is to be more biblically aware and to look at past and current legislation with critical respect.

A nation's laws reflect and perpetuate certain values and attitudes. This is a lesson to be drawn from Deuteronomy 4:5–8, which was cited earlier. The question that needs to be asked is: What does current immigration law say about this country's values and the kind of people we are? What sort of laws would communicate the ideals that the United States holds and would like other countries to admire? In addition, in terms of the structure of Paul's letter to the Romans, the Christian mind-set is established in chapter 12 (note 12:1–2), where we are commanded to take care even of our enemies (12:17–21). To submit to the laws of the land does not mean that these laws are all just or good for the country, nor does it mean that we cannot work for their reform. This Catholic-evangelical dialogue in many ways is an expression of dissatisfaction with parts of actual or potential US legislation and cultural trends. The democratic system of this country allows for such expressions of discontent and initiatives for change. The laws on immigration, I believe, fall within the category of those laws that need reform.

CONCLUSION AND BRIEF COMMENTS
ON PUBLIC POLICY IMPLICATIONS

There is much within the Bible that is relevant for the national debate, both for the host culture and the immigrant population. The Old and New Testaments demonstrate God's love for the vulnerable, and his commitment to displaced peoples is evident throughout. The challenge for Catholic and evangelical alike is to discern how these biblical perspectives and imperatives might find expression in their educational programs, worship, ministries, and institutions.

How all of this biblical teaching can be brought to bear on the broader society also is a complicated matter.[17] The Bible does not (and indeed cannot) offer a blueprint for public policy. Nevertheless, it does point the way to foundational moral principles that should govern Christian attitudes and behavior (individually and corporately) and can orient Christian participation in the public square (at whatever level and arena). Drawing from the biblical teaching on the value of every human being and the call for compassion and justice for the outsider, some recommendations are quite appropriate. Deliberations on specifics should include analyses of the multiple immigrant realities like those that were mentioned in the introductory section of this essay and that can be found in the sources cited in the footnotes. The following general recommendations, congruent with the biblical material, are those stated in the NAE resolution:

17. Of course, there are several church-state models that have been developed over the centuries in the various Christian traditions. My comments are of a more general nature.

- That immigrants be treated with respect and mercy by the Christian churches. Exemplary treatment of the immigrant by Christians can serve as the moral basis to call for government attitudes and legislation to reflect those same virtues.

- That the government develop structures and mechanisms that safeguard and monitor the national borders with efficiency and respect for human dignity.

- That the government establish more functional legal mechanisms for the annual entry of a reasonable number of immigrant workers and families.

- That the government recognize the central importance of the family in society by reconsidering the number and categories of visas available for family reunification, by dedicating more resources to reducing the backlog of cases in process, and by reevaluating the impact of deportation on families.

- That the government establish a sound, equitable process toward earned legal status for currently undocumented immigrants, who desire to embrace the responsibilities and privileges that accompany citizenship.

- That the government legislate fair labor and civil laws for all residing within the United States that reflect the best of this country's heritage.

- That immigration enforcement be conducted in ways that recognize the importance of due process of law, the sanctity of the human person, and the incomparable value of the family.

These are working principles that could move the immigration discussion forward in civil and constructive fashion and serve as guidelines for cooperation between Catholics and evangelicals. Our hope is that this essay's brief survey of what the Bible says about welcoming the stranger can lead to more informed Christian attitudes and stimulate concrete action on behalf of the immigrant.

APPENDIX: DENOMINATIONAL STATEMENTS ON IMMIGRATION

Note: This list is not exhaustive and is not limited to explicitly evangelical denominations. Many of these statements are positive toward immigrants as people, but less clear on national policy.

American Baptist Church:
  http://www.abc-usa.org/what_we_believe/mission/immigration-letter/
Assemblies of God: http://www.ag.org/top/About/immigration.cfm
Church of the Nazarene:
  http://www.usacanadaregion.org/ministries/multicultural-ministries/
  serving-immigrants
Evangelical Covenant Church: http://www.covchurch.org/resolutions/2006-
  immigration/
Evangelical Free Church:
  http://www.efca.org/reachnational/immigrant-hope-tm
Evangelical Lutheran Church in America:
  http://www.elca.org/Faith/Faith-and-Society/SocialMessages/
  Immigration?_ga=1.234742110.1164632819.1475784045
Lutheran Immigration and Refugee Service: http://www.lirs.org/act/issues/cir
National Association of Evangelicals:
  http://www.nae.net/government-relations/policy-resolutions/354-
  immigration-2009
  http://www.nae.net/fthn/immigration-reform
  http://evangelicalimmigrationtable.com
  http://worldrelief.net/immigrant-legal-services/legal-support-network
National Council of Christian Churches: http://www.ncccusa.org/
  immigration/immigpolicies.html
Presbyterian Church (USA): http://oga.pcusa.org/section/departments/
  immigration/
Reformed Church of America: https://www.rca.org/sslpage.aspx?pid=504
Southern Baptist Convention: http://www.sbc.net/resolutions/amResolution.
  asp?ID=1157
SBC Ethics and Religious Liberty Commission: http://erlc.com/resource-
  library/topic-index/immigration
United Methodist Church: http://www.umc.org/site/c.lwL4KnN1LtH/
  b.7766363/k.6ECD/The_Church_and_Immigration.htm;
  http://www.umc.org/site/apps/nlnet/content2.aspx?c=lwL4KnN1LtH&b
  =4951419&ct=6480715&notoc=1;

https://umc-gbcs.org/content/general/INTERFAITH_CIR_
STATEMENT.PDF

Wesleyan Church: https://www.wesleyan.org/237/a-wesleyan-view-of-
immigration

Broader Institutions and Coalitions in Support of Comprehensive
Immigration Reform:

http://cwsglobal.org/our-work/refugees-and-immigrants/

http://faithandimmigration.org/

http://www.interfaithimmigration.org/issues/immigration-reform/

http://sojo.net/topics/racial-and-social-justice/immigration

http://undocumented.tv/

7

What Is God's Dream? Reflections on Solidarity with Refugees and Displaced Persons[1]

Leo J. O'Donovan, SJ

International refugee policy is a twentieth-century development.[2] In 1921 the League of Nations established a High Commission for Refugees that was led by the Norwegian Fridjoft Nansen and became, when he died in 1930, the Nansen International Office for Refugees. In the 1930s the League also established a commission to represent German refugees, but it was woefully inadequate. When the two offices joined in 1938 and moved to London, they proved even less able to aid refugees from central Europe in a significant way.

The first post-World War II refugee cycle lasted from the war until the mid-1950s. During that decade, various United Nations organizations were established to assist populations displaced by the war as well as in Palestine

1. Some of the material in this essay was previously published in "Nous, les réfugiés: L'expérience du déracinement aujourd'hui," *Christus* (April 2011) 203–12.

2. For the following, cf. Richard Ryscavage, SJ, "Refugees Today: Rescue or Containment?," in *Who Are My Sisters and Brothers? Reflections on Understanding and Welcoming Immigrants and Refugees* (Washington, DC: United States Catholic Conference, 1996), 1–8; Susan F. Martin, "Rethinking the International Refugee Regime in Light of Human Rights and the Global Common Good," in David Hollenbach, ed., *Driven from Home: Protecting the Rights of Forced Migrants* (Washington, DC: Georgetown University Press, 2010), 15–33; Maryanne Loughry, "The Experience of Displacement by Conflict: The Plight of Iraqi Refugees," in David Hollenbach, ed., *Driven from Home: Protecting the Rights of Forced Migrant* (Washington, DC: Georgetown University Press, 2010), 169–83.

and Hong Kong.[3] Another important development was the 1948 adoption of the Universal Declaration of Human Rights (UDHR), for which, as we now know, Catholic social teaching provided a significant inspiration.[4] Most significant of all was the 1951 Convention Relating to the Status of Refugees (United Nations High Commissioner for Refugees [UNHCR]). According to the Convention, a refugee is any person who:

> owing to a well-founded fear of being persecuted for reasons of race, religion, nationality, membership in a particular social group or political opinion, is outside the country of his nationality and is unable—or owing to such fear, unwilling—to avail himself of the protection of the country; or who, not having a nationality and being outside the country of his former habitual residence as a result of such events, is unable, or owing to such fear, is unwilling to return to it.[5]

Four points here are key: only persons who have crossed an internationally recognized border are included; the persons are objectively at risk; fear of persecution is the motivation for movement; the risk the persons face results from race, religion, nationality, membership in a social group, or political opinion. A 1967 Protocol universalized this legal definition to include refugees at any time and anywhere in the world. (It had been restricted to European refugees before 1951.) According to the Convention, the central obligation of states is not to return (or *refoule*) refugees to the states they have fled.

A second refugee cycle began in the late 1950s and lasted to the mid-1970s. With most war refugees settled and the Soviet Union's hold on Eastern Europe preventing significant emigration (the failed Hungarian revolution was a major exception), the UNHCR's role came to include refugees in Africa and Asia whose flight was prompted less by persecution than by military violence, especially in the wars of liberation. In 1969 the recently established Organization of African Unity (OAU) adopted the Convention Governing the Specific Aspects of Refugee Problems in Africa, which addressed the new causes of refugee movement. In particular,

3. The United Nations Relief and Rehabilitation Administration (UNRRA, 1943); the International Refugee Organization (1946); the UN Relief and Work Administration (UNRWA, 1948).

4. Cf. Mary Ann Glendon, *A World Made New: Eleanor Roosevelt and the Universal Declaration of Human Rights* (New York: Random House, 2002) and "The Sources of 'Rights Talk,'" *Commonweal* (October 12, 2001) 11–13.

5. www.UNHCR.org/protect/PROTECTION/3b66c2aa10.pdf.

it forbade the rejection of asylum seekers at state borders, a point on which the UDHR had been silent.

From the mid-1970s through the late 1980s, the number of refugees, especially from the third world, increased dramatically. Regional conflicts and civil wars in Central America, Southeast Asia, and Southern Africa became surrogates for the Cold War between the superpowers. In 1984, the Organization of American States adopted the Cartagena Declaration on Refugees, based again on the 1951 Convention but recognizing the new grounds—violence, internal conflict, serious violations of human rights—for refugee flight.[6] Gradually it became common practice to accept as refugees those escaping conflict—even if they were at the same time actively opposing the regime they had fled.

With the fall of the Berlin Wall and of communism in the Soviet Union and Eastern Europe, a further refugee cycle began to confront international society. More refugees found it possible to return to their homelands, and Sadako Ogata, then the UNHCR, declared the 1990s "the decade of repatriation." But the hope for a new order was grievously belied by tragedies such as Bosnia, Kosovo, and Rwanda. The problem of internally displaced persons (IDPs, those forced to migrate within their own countries) became increasingly urgent. But none of the UN and humanitarian agencies that arose had a global mandate to protect and assist the internally displaced.[7]

Within the agencies involved, and academically as well, the debate continues as to who should be responsible for IDPs. The UNHCR has broadened its policy on internal displacement but has been warned not to become an IDP agency. In addition, the UNHCR has shown a willingness, beyond providing assistance for conflict IDPs, to assist forced migrations that result from natural disasters such as tsunamis and earthquakes. More recently still, displacements caused by climate change have been recognized as increasingly urgent.[8]

---

6. The goals of the declaration were, typically, protection, assistance, and repatriation.

7. Cf. Roberta Cohen and Francis Deng, *Masses in Flight: The Global Crisis of Internal Displacement* (Washington, DC: Brookings Institution, 1998).

8. Cf. António Guterres, "Millions Uprooted: Saving Refugees and the Displaced," *Foreign Affairs* Vol. 87, No. 5 (September/October 2008) 90–99, at 99.

MIGRANTS AND THEIR DEFENSE

To the immense number of forcibly displaced persons, whether internally or as refugees, an increasing number of immigrants warrants international attention and concern. Leaving their homeland not because of persecution or conflict but for economic opportunity, their situation in many respects resembles that of refugees and IDPs, particularly in the case of undocumented immigrants: economic uncertainty (and accompanying hardships), exploitation, disruption of families, deprivation of basic human rights (education, healthcare), and threatened cultural identity.

More than fifty years ago, Pope John XXIII's encyclical *Pacem in Terris* (1963) strongly affirmed the right of people to exercise their social and economic rights in their homelands but also to migrate if they could not support themselves at home (art. 25; cf. 106). The goods of the earth are destined not simply for those who presently enjoy them but for the human family as a whole. Just as private property is not an absolute but a relative right, so too states have the right to protect their borders for the common good of their people. But that right is relative to the more universal right of the world's poor and vulnerable to shelter and sustenance. In their joint pastoral letter "Strangers No Longer: Together on the Journey of Hope" (2003), the Bishops of Mexico and the United States put the point forcefully, emphasizing "the presumption of migration and reception over sovereignty in light of the contemporary situation of global poverty and persecution . . . [and asserting] that the right of a sovereign state to control its borders to promote the common good and the human right to migrate in order to realize God-given rights are complementary."[9]

With the number of refugees and other displaced persons at an all-time high in the world today (more than 65.3 million), and a current administration in the United States that sees the situation not as a humanitarian crisis

9. Kristin E. Heyer, "The Common Good and the American Bishops' Guidelines," in Richard W. Miller, ed., *We Hold These Truths: Catholicism and American Political Life* (Liguori, MO: Liguori, 2008), 45–62, at 60. "In Catholic teaching," summarizes Drew Christiansen, SJ, "the right of states to exclude immigration, though not necessarily to regulate it, is limited to special, exceptional circumstances. It ought not be a matter of general practice"—"Sacrament of Unity: Ethical Issues in Pastoral Care of Migrants and Refugees," in *Today's Immigrants and Refugees: A Christian Understanding* (Washington, DC: National Conference of Catholic Bishops, 1988), 81–114, at 89. The charter document on migrants is Pope Pius XII, *Exsul Familia* ("On the Spiritual Care of Migrants"), 1952. The right to emigrate is also affirmed in Paul VI's *Octogesima Adveniens* (1971, art. 17) and in John Paul II's *Laborem Exercens* (1981, art. 23).

but as grounds for fear, men and women of good will everywhere are called to ask what their fundamental human relationship to these people should be. For Christians this means a call to cultivate a spirituality of solidarity with people created, according to the book of Genesis as the very images of God and, according to the New Testament, as the brothers and sisters of Christ for whom he gave his life, from incarnation through the paschal mystery of cross and resurrection. Some liken the situation of refugees to that of all Christians, seeking a home that cannot be found in this world. They, like all of us, are pilgrims. But recognizing such similarities can quite easily incline us to feel absolved of our responsibilities in the present and desperate situation. It is likewise questionable whether the easy appropriation of a generalized concept of "exile," whether supposedly grounded in biblical or mystical witness, does either exiles or those called to stand with them a true service.

BIBLICAL FOUNDATIONS

As with social issues generally, the witness of Scripture remains definitive for Christians even while the significant contextual differences between the biblical period and our own need to be borne in mind—as regards the size of populations, the awareness of the responsibilities of international society, the development of increasing (though scarcely worldwide) commitment to universal human rights, and, within the Catholic Church, a steadily growing body of social teaching. The two defining moments in the history of the Jewish people, the Exodus and the Exile, led to powerful theologies of liberation, one testifying to God's deliverance of the people from enforced labor in Egypt and toward a promised land, the other lamenting enforced displacement in Babylon but celebrating the people's return to the land of the promise. Recalling the Exodus, God repeatedly commands the people to love the stranger and the alien, for they too had been strangers in a foreign land (Deut 19:19, Exod 23:9, Lev 19:33–34). As a providentially delivered people, they are called to loving hospitality, not merely as a social nicety but as a sacred necessity, mimicking the protective care of their Lord. "The alien who resides with you shall be to you as the citizen among you; you shall love the alien as yourself, for you were aliens in the land of Egypt: I am the Lord your God" (Lev 19:34).[10]

10. On the paradigmatic Old Testament stories concerning hospitality to strangers, cf. Patrick D. Miller Jr., "Israel as Host to Strangers," in *Today's Immigrants and Refugees*, 1–19, at 10.

Contemporary scholarship is increasingly suspicious of "the myth of exile and return." But the great exilic literature—Jeremiah, Ezekiel, and Second Isaiah—does respond to the threat to the people's very existence posed by the loss of the land where they had lived as the Lord's guests. It assures them that exile is not their final destiny (e.g., Jer 31:31–34). There will be a renewed temple in a renewed land (Ezek 40–48) and a new exodus from Babylon (Isa 40–55). Whatever the number of deportees to Babylon in the three successive deportations of 597, 586, and 582 BCE, and however many actually returned to Israel (there were surely many more in the Diaspora), Jewish memory and identity were stamped by what the Lord had done to punish a faithless people—but likewise by all that the Lord could redeem. This literature thus sees migration and exile as central, not peripheral, to biblical tradition; it argues for the transformation of what had been a curse into a blessing. Yet it also led to a heightened conviction of the people of God, suggests Leslie J. Hoppe, OFM, not as possessors of the land but as no more than resident aliens.[11]

Displacement is a central theme in the New Testament as well. The Holy Family flees the wrath of Herod as refugees to Egypt. Jesus conducts his ministry as an itinerant preacher "with nowhere to lay his head" (Luke 9:58). In the parable of the Great Judgment, he identifies himself implicitly with the stranger whom the righteous have welcomed (Matt 25:35). As he announces God's dwelling in time with lost human beings, he risks all to open an everlasting dwelling with God in the Holy Spirit—less a "return" than a final, perilous journey to the earthly Jerusalem of his crucifixion and *through* that to the heavenly Jerusalem of his resurrection. The Letter to the Hebrews celebrates him as the true high priest who has entered the heavenly sanctuary once and for all (a sanctuary created *through* his entering it). Having come from a people who "acknowledged that they were strangers and exiles on the earth . . . seeking a homeland [and] desir[ing] a better country, that is, a heavenly one" (Heb 11:13–15), he opened the way for their final, transcendent journey—and ours. Written at roughly the same time, the First Letter of Peter likewise speaks—probably metaphorically— of persecuted Christians in northern Asia Minor as exiles (1:1) and urges them "as aliens and exiles to abstain from the passions of the flesh that wage war against your soul (2:11)." (Eph 2:12–22 has, however, a noticeably different perspective.)

11. Cf. Leslie J. Hoppe, OFM, "Israel Experiences Exile," in *Today's Immigrants and Refugees*, 21–42, at 23.

As a multidimensional metaphor, resonant with other fundamental human experiences such as community disruption, homelessness, and confusion in personal identity, not to mention social, cultural, and economic deprivations, the theme of exile has repeatedly been used to express Christianity's situation in the world. The "Letter to Diognetus" is perhaps its classic statement. The theme also occurs in the prayer of mystics and the piety of everyday Christians. (The *Salve Regina,* singing of "the exiled children of Eve . . . mourning and weeping in this valley of tears," is typical). The Second Preface of Christmas looks to Christ coming "to lead humankind from exile into [God's] heavenly kingdom." But interestingly the theme is not frequent in the texts of Vatican II, although it does occur in three documents, notably in the Dogmatic Constitution on the Church, which speaks of the church as journeying "in a foreign land away from the Lord . . . [and] see[ing] herself as an exile" (6.)

MIRACULOUS MULTIFORMITY

In many parts of the church today, its bishops have borne eloquent witness to our responsibilities in the current crisis. Over a decade ago, for example, a joint pastoral letter from the Bishops of Mexico and the United States, "Strangers No Longer: Together on the Journey of Hope" (2003), emphasized that in the contemporary situation of global poverty and persecution the reception of migrants is a moral claim that must be considered at the same time as national sovereignty in its usual sense. Ethicists such as David Hollenbach and Kristin Heyer have developed this fundamental principle that the right of a sovereign state to control its borders to promote the common good and the human right to migrate in order to realize God-given rights are not antithetical but complementary.

Other theologians who have recently addressed the plight of refugees as well as internally displaced persons are in the first place concerned with protection, care, and justice for them. The Jesuit Refugee service, for example, summarizes its mission as accompaniment, service, and advocacy. There is a significant theology to be mined here. Migrants may first be thought of as "other" and "strange" in a receiving culture. But they can also bear with them new human resources and experiences, reminding the receiving culture of the miraculous multiformity of the human family in God's creation. As Senator George Mitchell recently remarked: "Three of the most valuable and successful business enterprises in the world are Apple,

Amazon, and Google. Apple was created by Steve Jobs, whose father was born in Syria. Amazon was created by Jeff Bezos, whose adoptive father was born in Cuba. And a cofounder of Google was Sergey Brin, who was born in Russia."[12] In addition, of the seven Americans who won Nobel prizes in 2016, six are immigrants (winning in chemistry, physics, and economics).

Can a country founded on immigration learn to appreciate our new immigrants? It requires not the counsels of intimidating fear but the conversion of open hearts. And as the US and Mexican bishops wrote in the document I quoted earlier: "Part of the process of conversion of mind and heart deals with confronting attitudes of cultural superiority, indifference and racism; accepting migrants not as foreboding aliens, terrorists, or economic threats, but as persons with dignity and rights, revealing the presence of Christ; and recognizing migrants as bearers of deep cultural values and rich faith traditions."[13]

SOLIDARITY IN CREATION AND VOCATION

The eyes of faith in a crucified Christ can see Christ in the refugee and the refugee in Christ. The displacement suffered by so many people today continues the *via crucis*, "filling up the sufferings of Christ" as his incarnation gathers the human family into itself.[14] A church called to announce good news to all times and places is called to identify with the displaced but finds that the displaced also identify the church to itself, learning to realize that it is essentially migrant, never arriving in this world at the "rest of God" that is eschatologically promised to it.[15]

This new theology of displacement deepens what we mean by creation, by Christ as our savior, by the church as the people of God, and by our hope for "a new heaven and a new earth." But in its admirable solidarity with the displaced it needs also to be critical of metaphors such as exile, which prove to be inherently ambiguous and easily misleading. Exile and displacement are the result of sociopolitical, economic, and now, increasingly, ecological causes. They are not an inevitable destiny (and certainly not God's will) but rather injustice that calls out for redress.[16]

12. *America* vol. 216, no. 6 (March 20, 2017) 54.

13. *Strangers No Longer*, no. 40.

14. Cf. Col 1:24.

15. Heb 4:11.

16. Cf. Gustavo Gutiérrez, "Poverty, Migration, and the Option for the Poor," in

Few events of the last half century have so fiercely embodied and sadly symbolized the plight of displaced people as have the walls built in Berlin, Israel, and, to the great regret of many Americans, along the Southwest border between the United States and Mexico. The "fence," as it was first euphemistically called, was begun by the Department of Homeland Security in November 2005 against illegal drugs and immigration. It was coupled with a "Secure Border Initiative" (later cancelled by the Obama administration) based on surveillance towers and wireless communication. By January 2010, at an estimated cost of $3 million a mile, 670 miles of fence had been built (the entire border stretches 2,000 miles).

Now, in fulfillment of Mr. Trump's signature campaign pledge, the administration's proposed budget includes billions of dollars for the design and construction of the wall. Additional funds are designated to hire new personnel in the departments of Justice and Homeland Security, as well as for the deportation of undocumented immigrants. $1.5 billion is allocated for new detention facilities. The overall estimated cost of a completed wall ranges from $12 to $21 billion, meant to be covered by radical cuts elsewhere in the budget.

Strong opposition has been voiced against a wall from the beginning: on economic grounds (its great expense, cost overruns, the disruption of local economies); as an ineffective deterrent (the Border Patrol estimated that it apprehends only one out of every four or five crossers and currently the great majority of undocumented immigrants are visa-overstayers); for environmental and cultural reasons (it runs through the tribal lands of three American Indian nations as well as the University of Texas at Brownsville); above all, for inappropriately endangering the lives of migrants, thousands of whom have died in the desert.

The current administration's fear-mongering distortions of reality, both human and economic, have as their chief spokesman Attorney General Jeff Sessions. In Holy Week of 2017, Mr. Sessions visited the Arizona border and pronounced it a "ground zero" of death and violence where Americans must "take our stand" against the supposed criminals and rapists against whom our current president inveighed in his presidential campaign. What *The New York Times* editorial page called Mr. Sessions's "gonzo-apocalyptic

Daniel G. Groody and Gioacchino Campese, eds., *A Promised Land, A Perilous Journey* (Notre Dame, IN: University of Notre Dame Press, 2008), 76–86. Also Gutiérrez, *The Power of the Poor in History* (Maryknoll, NY: Orbis, 1983).

vision of immigration"[17] misleads the public on multiple counts. For twenty years illegal border crossings from Mexico have been declining. Talk of "war zones" is wholly incommensurate with the actual entering immigrants whom ICE finds fleeing acute violence in increasingly desperate countries in Central America. Such people are in fact less likely to commit crimes than are native-born American citizens. The economic contributions of millions of the unauthorized have been manifold. Many of them have lived peaceably in the United States for a decade or more. And they certainly pose no real threat to the job security of workers in Wisconsin, Michigan, or Pennsylvania who are suffering, and indeed very painfully, from the obsolescence of their industries. Finally, and crucially, polls show that increasing numbers of Americans favor practical, humane immigration reform. They are learning to remember where they came from.[18]

What change of heart might lead Americans to recognize that the proposed, impractical wall is a cross from which refugees and migrants should be taken down?[19] Daniel G. Groody, CSC, suggests a theology and spirituality of migration (or of the displaced generally) that rests on four traditional and yet newly revealed foundations.[20] The first is the conception of human beings as *imago Dei*, as images of God in the world. As such, they cannot be adequately identified through purely legal, social, and political categories, in particular such prejudicial terms as "illegal alien." They are in

17. *The New York Times,* April 14, 2017. Equally apocalyptic was Homeland Security Secretary John Kelly in his first substantial address on the duties of his vast bureaucracy. "Make no mistake," he said during a speech at George Washington University on April 18. "We are in fact a nation under attack." *The New York Times,* April 21, 2017.

18. Cf. Kristin E. Heyer, "Social Sin and Immigration: Good Fences Make Bad Neighbors," *Theological Studies* vol. 71, no. 2 (June 2010) 410–36.

19. Cf. Ignacio Ellacuria, "The Crucified People," in Ignacio Ellacuria and Jon Sobrino, eds., *Mysterium Liberationis: Fundamental Concepts of Liberation Theology* (Maryknoll, NY: Orbis, 1993), 580–603. For commentary: Gioacchino Campese, "¿Cuanto Más? The Crucified People at the U.S.-Mexico Border," in eds. Groody and Campese, *A Promised Land, A Perilous Journey,* 271–98.

20. Daniel G. Groody, CSC, "Crossing the Divide: Foundations of a Theology of Migration and Refugees," *Theological Studies* vol. 70, no. 3 (September 2009) 638–67. Republished in Donald Kerwin and Jill Marie Gerschutz, eds., *And You Welcomed Me: Migration and Catholic Social Teaching* (Lanham, MD: Lexington, 2009). Among Groody's many other publications, see also "La foi sur la frontière ou la 'migration' comme métaphore de la vie spirituelle," *Lumen Vitae* vol. 59, issue 4 (December 2004) 441–52; "A Theology of Migration," *America* vol. 204, no. 3 (February 7, 2011) 18–20; "Passing Over: Migration as Conversion," *International Review of Mission* vol. 104, issue 1 (April 2015) 46–61.

the first place bearers of inalienable human rights, intersubjectively related to their fellow human beings and to the mystery of God.

Redeemed by the *Verbum Dei* incarnate, every man and woman shares as well the human condition that Jesus of Nazareth risked everything to save. They are newly born, newly called together to a final communion with the saints in God that transcends all national borders and identities. "Through the *Verbum Dei*," Groody has written, "Jesus' *kenosis* and death on the cross, God overcomes the barriers caused by sin, redraws the borders created by people who have withdrawn from God, and enters into the most remote and abandoned places of the human condition."[21]

Further, it is the mission of the church, God's own mission, to bring to all peoples the hope of restoration to their full dignity as images of God redeemed by the paschal mystery of Christ. Here the migratory character of Christian existence, its call to move always beyond any settled place, is perhaps clearest. (Groody also offers helpful insights on the notion of "illegality," drawing on Thomistic theology and Catholic social teaching that distinguishes between various kinds of law: divine, eternal, natural, and civil—distinctions that concern how fundamental a given law is and that are all too easily overlooked in discussions about the "status" of the displaced.)

The fourth, encompassing foundation is the *visio Dei*, understood as the saving vision of the kingdom of God. Read and reconsidered in the light of the experience of migrants and refugees, the promise of this vision is at once a source of hope, a ground for courage, and a consolation that in no way distracts from social and political engagement. Rather, it gives such engagement its deepest justification and purpose.

This kind of theology of migration, as I have said, can renew our theology of creation, Christology, ecclesiology, and eschatology. It also alerts us to the signs of spiritualizing the good news of God's coming to and in the displaced. A false spirituality disregards the enormous inequities of the distribution of wealth in the world. It acquiesces all too easily to the purported inevitability of violence and war. It is often accompanied by a resigned acceptance of the arms race and nuclear proliferation. It is disinterested in the question of climate change. And it considers "a community of nations" to be a merely utopian vision. Yet all these attitudes stand in direct contradiction to the social teaching of popes and bishops and countless grassroots organizations in the Catholic church.

21. Groody, "Crossing the Divide," 649.

BELONGING TO EACH OTHER

A truth as old as it is new may serve to focus in a central way the emerging theology and spirituality of refugees, migrants, and all the displaced. It is this: The body which the Holy Spirit is building in Christ for God is *one* body, and we are all, we vulnerable and yet victorious members of Christ, all members likewise of each other. The image is more than an image. It is a fundamental vision which we can appreciate still more today as not merely moral but ontological—the way things are. From Paul through the Patristic period and on to modern papal teaching, the *project* of one human family in which all depend on and belong to each other has become bedrock realism for Christianity. And so displacement and exile for fellow human beings is less a sign of what may come to be than a definition of who we ourselves presently are. It may be a way of understanding the church, but only insofar as the people of the church realize themselves as one with and belonging to those members who now suffer displacement. Such a personal and social realism, it seems to me, is indispensable for grounding a Christianity that serves the transformation of its world—as well as the ground for a practical spirituality of solidarity with refugees *in the present*.

We are all displaced now, all refugees. What can be done about it? "What is God's dream?" as Francisco Herrera, a long-time California advocate for immigrant rights, has put it. "That's what we need to ask."[22]

---

22. Quoted in Robert Wuthnow, *All in Sync: How Music and Art Are Revitalizing American Religion* (Berkeley, CA: University of California Press, 2003), 202.

8

Racial Reconciliation and the Pro-Life Agenda: An African American Perspective

CHERYL J. SANDERS

INTRODUCTION

In his 1987 book *Completely Pro-Life*, evangelical theologian Ron Sider advocated a "biblically informed pro-life agenda" that seeks fullness of life for everyone, including the unborn and those marginalized in any way.[1] Twenty-five years later in *Just Politics: A Guide for Christian Engagement*, Sider observed that "increasingly, Christians are embracing this broader agenda."[2] He sees the center of Catholicism and white evangelicalism now advocating a pro-life, pro-poor, pro-family, pro-social justice, pro-sexual integrity, and pro-creation care agenda. But what about African American Christians? Does a "completely pro-life" agenda also represent the thinking of a majority of African Americans?

While African American and white evangelicals both hold the Bible in high regard, many African American Christians adhere to a reading of the Bible that is theologically conservative and politically progressive at

1. Ronald J. Sider, *Completely Pro-Life: Building a Consistent Stance* (Downers Grove, IL: InterVarsity, 1987), 189.

2. Ronald J. Sider, *Just Politics: A Guide for Christian Engagement* (Grand Rapids: Brazos, 2012), 126.

the same time. This reading supports heterosexual, monogamous marriage and a God who favors the poor and delivers people from slavery and oppression. It upholds the example of Jesus as a mandate for the church to preach good news to the poor and make disciples of all nations, supported by ministries of healing and reconciliation. This view of the Scriptures and the church is consistent with a pro-life agenda but opposes political indifference to poverty and social injustice.

One reason that African Americans and whites may differ in their embrace of a pro-life agenda is that many African Americans doubt the willingness of whites to acknowledge the value of black life outside the womb. In other words, the ongoing impact of the problem of race on the sanctity of human life imposes a huge dilemma upon African American Christians. The perceived indifference of many white Americans to poverty and hunger as public policy issues may cause African Americans to question the integrity of the pro-life agenda of white evangelicals, notwithstanding the moral presumptions African Americans may bring to their opposition to abortion. The task at hand is renewed advocacy of a progressive pro-life agenda that ascribes the same value to black lives as to others at every stage of development, with a consistent focus on elevating quality of life and equality of opportunity for all.

RACIAL IDENTITY AND AMERICAN POLITICS: THE ELEPHANT IN THE ROOM

The media coverage of the 2012 political conventions and election night results presented some ironic and compelling portrayals. In the summer of 2012, the two political conventions projected two radically different images—an overwhelmingly white gathering convened by the Republican Party to nominate Gov. Mitt Romney on the one hand, and the broad diversity of the Democratic Convention on the other. On election night in November 2012, the television networks cut back and forth between images of the diverse and exuberant crowd dancing as they awaited the delayed delivery of President Barack Obama's acceptance speech at McCormick Place in Chicago and the somber assembly of well-heeled white supporters who sobbed in a Boston hotel in woeful anticipation of a concession speech from a reluctant Gov. Romney. Four years later, there was an ironic reversal in the portraits of election night celebrations by Democrats and Republicans, this time both assembled in the heart of New York City. This time the diverse audience of Democrats wept in shock and dismay as the reality sunk in that Hilary Clinton, former First Lady, US Senator, and Secretary of State, had won the popular vote but failed to capture a sufficient number of electoral votes to be elected the first female President of the US. The nation was kept waiting until the middle of the following day to hear her concession speech. This time the Republicans were exuberant in victory throughout the night as a nearly all-white audience celebrated the triumph of Republican candidate Donald Trump, a billionaire real estate developer and reality television star whose key campaign slogan was to "Make America Great Again," mainly by deporting illegal immigrants and Muslims and by reinstating manufacturing jobs that have been exported overseas. The key constituencies who secured Trump's victory were white Christians: white evangelicals (81 percent), white Protestants (58 percent), and white Catholics (60 percent). By contrast, 88 percent of black voters supported Clinton.[3]

Reflecting upon these voting patterns in the last two presidential elections, it is clear that the vast majority of white evangelicals supported Republican candidates and policies, while African American Christians have stood firm in their commitment to the Democratic Party, notwithstanding the pro-choice stance regarding abortion and marriage equality embraced by both Obama and Clinton. Many African American voters frowned upon Trump's bigoted speeches and were hardly persuaded by Trump's pitch to black voters: "what the hell do you have to lose?" Any objections African American Christians may have had to the social liberalism of the Democratic Party were clearly outweighed by their rejection of the messages Trump crafted to appeal to the anger and resentments of white Christians. For many African Americans, the promise to make American great again was heard as the deep-seated intention to make America white again, fueled by the resentment of having been governed for eight years by a black president. Trump's lack of credibility among African American voters stands in stark contrast to his broad appeal to white Christians, whose enthusiasm for Trump was undeterred by his multiple marriages, numerous allegations of sexual misconduct, lewd language with reference to women, ridicule of disabled persons, insulting and derogatory comments about his opponents, and his complete lack of experience and expertise in politics. These same white voters rejected Clinton's appeals for unity, diversity, and

3. Lauren Markoe, "White evangelicals, Catholics and Mormons carried Trump," *Religion News Service*, November 9, 2016; and Tami Luhby and Jennifer Agiesta, "CNN Exit polls: Clinton fails to energize African-Americans, Latinos and the young," *CNN Politics*, November 9, 2016.

equality, instead buying into Trump's characterization of her as "crooked Hilary" because of her deleted emails.

For more than five centuries, generations of African American Christians have complained of the persistent and hypocritical racism of white Christians who promoted slavery and the slave trade; colonized Africa, South America, and the Caribbean; and endorsed racial discrimination and injustice in the US. So any effort to unite African American and white Christians along the lines of a pro-life agenda must begin by addressing the "elephant in the room," namely, the failure of white Christians to reject the politics of racism and bigotry and embrace people of "color" as equal participants in the church and society. How can we account for the inability of Christians to perceive the injustice of these practices as an ungodly affront to the human dignity of others?

HOWARD THURMAN AND THE RELIGION OF JESUS

For a thoughtful answer to this critical question, we can turn to the testimony of Howard Thurman, the most influential African American theologian of the twentieth century. He tells the story of his 1935 visit to Ceylon as a young minister and scholar, when during a conversation over coffee he was confronted by the principal of a law college who challenged Thurman to defend his Christian faith as a black American:

> You have lived in a Christian nation in which you are segregated, lynched, and burned. Even in the church, I understand, there is segregation. One of my students who went to your country sent me a clipping telling about a Christian church in which the regular Sunday worship was interrupted so that many could join a mob against one of your fellows. When he had been caught and done to death, they came back to resume their worship of their Christian God. I am a Hindu. I do not understand. Here you are in my country, standing deep within the Christian faith and tradition. I do not wish to seem rude to you. But, sir, I think you are a traitor to all the darker peoples of the earth.[4]

In 1949 Thurman published an account of his measured response to this affront in a small but influential book, *Jesus and the Disinherited*. He proclaims the significance of the religion of Jesus to "people who stand with

4. Howard Thurman, *Jesus and the Disinherited* (Boston: Beacon; reprint ed., 1996), 14–15.

their backs against the wall," and he offers a line of questioning that bears directly on the current potential for meaningful interracial dialogue among Christians:

> This is the question which individuals and groups who live in our land always under the threat of profound social and psychological displacement face: Why is it that Christianity seems impotent to deal radically, and therefore effectively, with the issues of discrimination and injustice on the basis of race, religion, and national origin? Is this impotency due to a betrayal of the genius of the religion, or is it due to a basic weakness in the religion itself?[5]

In his book Thurman portrays Jesus as an impoverished Jew living under conditions of political and economic oppression in a Palestinian homeland crushed under the heel of the Roman Empire. Thurman's defense of his own Christian faith is based on the simple logic that he is a follower of Jesus, who was absolutely truthful in his witness against the same forces of poverty, oppression, and injustice experienced by Thurman's own people in his own time and social location. Encounters with God aboard the slave ships—under brutal conditions and endless humiliations of forced servitude—brought forth songs of lament and triumph known as the Negro spirituals. Out of deep suffering emerged hope for a future where freedom and justice would prevail, not just in the afterlife but also on earth for the benefit of generations to come. Throughout his lifetime, Thurman vigorously devoted his best intellectual energies and spiritual resources to fostering racial reconciliation and social change in the US and abroad.

Thurman's story embodies the spiritual and ethical legacy of African American Christians—their lament of the moral failings of the white Christians who victimized black people, their prayers to God to look with favor upon the poor in their affliction, and their celebration of God's power to bring justice and deliverance to the world. This perspective on faith and life is informed by the Bible, especially the Old Testament history, psalms, and prophets, and the New Testament gospels and epistles, notwithstanding the fact that during slavery African Americans in most states were by law deprived of access to literacy, education, and freedom of assembly for worship. A century and a half after the end of slavery, the only one of these three that has been effectively remedied is freedom to worship. Black denominations emerged during and after the slave era, not because of doctrinal disagreements but rather because white Christians

5. Ibid., Preface.

insisted upon imposing the color line in all aspects of social life, most notably in their places of worship. Racial profiling prevails in our cities, suburbs, and churches—that is, instantaneous negative judgments of persons based upon skin color, hairstyles, and apparel. Too many unarmed African Americans have been shot and killed with impunity by police officers. As long as this situation persists in the public consciousness, and as long as Thurman's question concerning the failure of Christians to address issues of discrimination and injustice remains unanswered, the problem of race will remain the chief factor accounting for differences in pro-life concepts between black and white Christians.

RECONCILIATION AND HOPE
IN THE BELOVED COMMUNITY

Is there any hope for achieving a unified agenda of religion and politics for North American Christians? Sociologists Michael O. Emerson and Christian Smith thoroughly investigated the problem of race and religion in the United States in their 2001 book, *Divided by Faith: Evangelical Religion and the Problem of Race in America.*[6] Based upon their surveys of 2,000 white evangelicals, they pinpointed some social blind spots that have caused white evangelicals to deny the problem of race and dismiss the agenda of racial reconciliation set forth by a few African Americans and whites after the death of Dr. Martin Luther King Jr. Smith and Emerson conclude that white evangelicals' emphasis upon individualism, free will, and personal relationships enables them to refuse to admit or acknowledge the sin of racial privilege. This problem could be alleviated by building personal relationships between blacks and whites, but these relationships are hindered by the reality of racial segregation in our communities and congregations. To make things worse, in the absence of regular interaction with blacks as neighbors or fellow church members, negative media stereotypes of blacks as criminals and buffoons further deprive whites of the opportunity to revise their attitudes toward blacks based upon personal relationships.

In 2012 Emerson partnered with Jason E. Shelton, an African American sociologist, to produce a comprehensive, systematic analysis of African American religious beliefs and political attitudes. This book, *Blacks and Whites in Christian America: How Racial Discrimination Shapes Religious*

---

6. Michael O. Emerson and Christian Smith, *Divided by Faith: Evangelical Religion and the Problem of Race in America* (New York: Oxford University Press, 2001).

Convictions, shows how the religious beliefs and practices of African Americans are shaped by the experience of racial discrimination. Shelton and Emerson report that while black Protestants strongly support opportunity-enhancing and outcome-based policies designed to assist African Americans with overcoming the problems of racial inequality, the vast majority of white Protestants neither support government efforts to assist minorities and the poor nor possess a strong commitment to social justice.[7] These authors use the term "identity politics" to explain the political partisanship of African American Protestants and white evangelicals, defining it as "the political beliefs and actions that are associated with a group of people that someone identifies with." Their study demonstrates how strong commitment to identity politics by both groups drives significant racial differences with respect to faith-based thoughts and practices.[8]

Shelton and Emerson acknowledge the continued importance of King's vision of the Beloved Community as a governing influence for African American Protestants. However, they caution that King's ideal of a "spiritually based gathering of people from all walks of life motivated by goodwill, reconciliation, and justice" will remain unachievable until Christians engage in "honest and forthright dialogue on the respective roles that racial oppression and privilege have played in shaping commitments to dissimilar models of Christianity."[9]

King's vision of the Beloved Community was incorporated into the racial reconciliation movement that emerged in the immediate aftermath of the civil rights movement. The first wave of this racial reconciliation movement was pioneered by a handful of black preachers, including John Perkins, Tom Skinner, and Samuel Hines, who argued that racism is a sin that should be viewed in the same way that Christians view other moral transgressions such as murder, theft, and adultery. They also proclaimed that black and white Christians must demonstrate God's power by not only reconciling to one another but also linking arms to fight against inequality and injustice.[10]

---

7. Jason E. Shelton and Michael O. Emerson, *Blacks and Whites in Christian America: How Racial Discrimination Shapes Religious Convictions* (New York: NYU Press, 2012), 4, 196–197.

8. Ibid., 4.

9. Ibid.

10. Ibid., 181.

The second wave of the racial reconciliation movement was popularized by white evangelical preachers and activists like Billy Graham and Promise Keepers founder Bill McCartney.[11] The second-wave reconciliation movement spawned new organizations, books, musicians, articles, publications, formal apologies, sermons, instructional guides, and religious conferences that addressed the issue. Promise Keepers events drew crowds of white evangelical men numbering in the hundreds of thousands to the National Mall in Washington, DC, and to the nation's largest stadiums and arenas. However, as the authors observe, the second wave fizzled out by the late 1990s due in part to its lack of a structural agenda for social change. Left in its wake were the masses of black and white evangelicals clinging to a divisive identity politics that has carried forcefully into the present century. Based on their findings, Shelton and Emerson are not particularly hopeful about the future: "Our quantitative and qualitative results suggest that contrasting commitments to identity politics severely limit prospects for racial reconciliation among black and white Protestants."[12] They express the clear conviction that, "in the final analysis, we cannot expect to live in a better world if we do not become actively involved in efforts to eliminate racism, poverty, and injustice."[13] Sadly, the fact that none of these issues were addressed in the 2016 presidential election underscores the patent unwillingness of the majority of white evangelicals and Catholics to join forces with African American Christians as witnesses for justice and reconciliation in the public square.

CONCLUSION

With four out of five white evangelical Christian voters approving the ascendancy of Donald Trump as president of the United States, identity politics has ushered our North American churches and society into an unprecedented era of racial conflict and political uncertainty. It is undeniable that the present political climate obscures the possibility that the white Christians who support him and the African American Christians who are offended by him will ever be able to come together in purposeful implementation of a pro-life agenda that is fully aligned with Dr. King's vision of the Beloved Community. Regardless of what it is called and who sets it in

11. Ibid., 182.
12. Ibid., 30.
13. Ibid., 207.

motion, the emergence of a renewed evangelical faith marked more by social justice than by identity politics will be necessary to sustain any shared vision of the common good. Moreover, the redemption of the troubled soul of a divided nation will require recovery of the potency of a Christian faith that, recalling the words of Howard Thurman, deals radically and effectively with the issues of discrimination and injustice on the basis of race, religion, and national origin.[14]

14. Thurman, *Jesus and the Disinherited,* Preface.

9

Honoring the Sacredness of Life in Public: An Evangelical Reflection

DAVID P. GUSHEE

INTRODUCTION

THE PURPOSE OF THIS chapter is to reflect on evangelical and Catholic efforts to bear public witness in the United States to what we believe about the sacredness of human life.

Everything about this topic is contested: what it means to speak in public as Christians; what it means to say that human life is sacred; what range of issues this purported sacredness might cover; whether it is appropriate for evangelicals, Catholics, and other people of faith to speak about the sacredness of life in the public square; whether doing so, even if constitutionally appropriate, is wise in terms of the broader Christian mission; and if so, what strategies we should pursue in advancing our goals.

I will take these questions in order, working my way through them so that by the end, what might result is at least a sketch of how centrist evangelicals and Catholics might understand and undertake public witness together on behalf of the sacredness of life.

SPEAKING IN PUBLIC AS CHRISTIANS

Perhaps the first thing to be said is that for Christians, reflection on and articulation of our ethical convictions begins as an ecclesial act and takes place within the Christian community/ies of which we are a part. British ethicist Nigel Biggar rightly points out that "for the Christian ethicist, the proper well-being of churches will have . . . priority" in our efforts.[1] He means that before we turn to broader public audiences such as nations, our task is to "shape the lives of churches and their members directly."[2]

Thus, before we bear any kind of public witness about a Christian conviction like the sacredness of life, our prior task is that "private" or "ecclesial public only" deliberative process in the church, in which we clarify our own Christian understanding of what this concept means and what its implications are for our own conduct. The Christian church, here understood broadly as the church universal, is a community of people pledged to Jesus Christ as Lord. We live under Christ's authority and therefore are obligated to a perpetual quest to determine what Christ wants us to believe and more importantly how he wants us to live. This we have done in a continuous stream of history extending nearly 2,000 years. We have undertaken this task in every different kind of political context and with every different level of visibility and social power, from the catacombs in hiding to the pinnacle of power. No human regime or worldly power authorizes our internal Christian moral discernment process, and none can prevent it. But likewise no political power on Earth is obligated in principle to hear, heed, or implement our moral convictions.

It is important to remind ourselves about the real distinction between speaking as Christians "among ourselves" about what we most truly believe, and turning to the broader public with a word for others, because such a distinction remains vulnerable to being effaced in many Christian circles.[3]

---

1. Biggar, *Behaving in Public* (Grand Rapids: Eerdmans, 2011), 46.

2. Ibid., 46–47.

3. Sometimes we are speaking privately, just among ourselves, and intending to do so, and yet broader audiences "overhear" our deliberations. Thus, for example, when a Christian body deliberates about what we should teach and do about the role of women in the church, or the moral legitimacy of non-marital sex for Christ's disciples, or the proper Christian stance toward wealth, sometimes our reflections "go public" even when we are not intending to make them public or seeking any kind of public impact. This is especially the case in our wired world in which cameras or computers capture nearly every waking moment in technologically advanced societies. While we should be aware of this overhearing phenomenon, and its positive and negative ramifications, this is still

One reason for this is that for almost 1,500 years, longer in some places, Christians grew accustomed to living in political regimes in which many of the moral convictions that arose out of the Christian faith were made into public law. We also became accustomed to cultures in which Christianity had no serious competition for shaping the social ethos, in part because other alternatives were suppressed or subordinated—often shamefully, and forcibly—to the prevailing Christian regime. This pattern was carried with Europeans into the colonial era and went everywhere Europeans went, including to colonial America.

Of course, we know that for a very interesting variety of reasons, not the least of which was the irreducible pluralism of Christian (and other) religions in late eighteenth century America after the revolution, the US First Amendment disestablished religion. There would be no official religion recognized by the government of the United States. There would be no official Christian power to enshrine Christian moral convictions into public law. After 1791, Christians in the United States could no longer count on the power of the state to advance Christian moral convictions.

But in retrospect it is clear that for most of American history the cultural (rather than political) hegemony of Christianity—especially Protestant Christianity—meant that whatever Christians arrived at in their personal or ecclesial moral discernment processes retained considerable cultural influence and quite often considerable legal weight. The influence of Christian convictions remained visible in local and national legislation on everything from marriage law to Sunday "blue laws" to the role of prayer in schools to the schedule of nationally recognized holidays.

It is only in the last few decades that the dramatic rise of religious pluralism and the growing ascendancy of an aggressive anti-religious secularism have clipped the wings of Christian cultural power in the United States. Though there is considerable local and regional variation, the United States is now a nation in which the easy assumption that Christian convictions would be influential in shaping public law no longer holds. This new reality has evoked a great deal of resentment on the part of many Christians, because no one likes to watch their power decline and, in a more generous reading, because Christians do not like the kind of national ethos we see developing amidst the weakening of Christian influence. One way to read the "culture wars" in the US is as the reflection of a grinding struggle for

not the same as when the church turns its face intentionally to the broader public and seeks a hearing for its ethical witness.

cultural power between a declining, but still large number of people seeking to retain the values of the older "Judeo-Christian" ethos over against a smaller but rapidly rising number of folks seeking to dethrone those values once and for all.

Today, then, when Christians who agree with each other about an idea like the sacredness of human life speak in public about it, we do so with uncertain effect. We do not have the political power to be sure that we can succeed in enshrining our dearest convictions into law. We encounter a context in which what we believe, and how we arrive at that belief, no longer make sense to many people; indeed, it arouses fierce opposition in some cases. The opposition is intense enough to create profound disdain for Christianity on the part of those most opposed. This in turn not only affects our likelihood of winning hearts, minds, and votes, but also raises profound questions about the impact of Christian public ethical witness on the broader reception of the Gospel message in American culture. This leads to the missional question as to whether Christians might consider downplaying our ethical witness in order to leave room for a more positive cultural response to the good news that God was in Christ reconciling the world to himself (2 Cor 5:17). But it might be that certain Christian moral convictions simply are so central that they cannot be downplayed for any reason. Or it might be that part of what we believe when we affirm certain Christian moral norms is that they apply not only to ourselves, but to everyone, that they are fundamental to a decent social order, and that therefore it is impossible to believe what we do without declaring it in public.

That, of course, is what most evangelicals and Catholics believe about a conviction we share called "the sacredness of human life."

WHAT IT MEANS TO SAY THAT HUMAN LIFE IS SACRED

I became so taken with this concept that human life is sacred that I spent seven years writing a book on the subject.[4] With the benefit of that work, I suggest that when Christians say human life is sacred, we mean:

God has consecrated each and every human being—without exception and in all circumstances—as a unique, incalculably precious being of elevated status and dignity. Through God's revelation in Scripture and incarnation in Jesus Christ, God has declared and demonstrated the sacred worth of human beings and will hold us accountable for responding appropriately. Such

4. Gushee, *The Sacredness of Human Life* (Grand Rapids: Eerdmans, 2013).

a response begins by adopting a posture of reverence and by accepting respon-sibility for the sacred gift that is a human life. It includes offering due respect and care to each human being that we encounter. It extends to an obligation to protect human life from wanton destruction, desecration, or the violation of human rights. A full embrace of the sacredness of human life leads to a full-hearted commitment to foster human flourishing.[5]

Notice a few important features of the sacredness of human life as I have just outlined it:

1) This conviction is intrinsically theological and deeply theocentric. To say that human life is sacred is to say that it has been consecrated by God.

2) This conviction is universalistic. To say that human life is sacred is to say that *each and every human being* is a being of elevated status and dignity in God's sight.

3) This conviction is grounded in the sources of the Christian tradition, notably Scripture and the incarnation. To say that human life is sacred is to reflect an aspect of divine revelation.

4) This conviction demands appropriate human moral response, sum-marized as reverence, responsibility, and respect for every human life. To say that human life is sacred is to require human beings to act as if the life of everyone is sacred.

5) This conviction demands, more specifically, efforts to prevent the desecration and destruction of human life and efforts to advance hu-man flourishing. To say that human life is sacred is to require human beings to prevent harm to people and to advance not just survival but human wholeness.

Most Christians to whom I have offered this rendering of the sacred-ness of human life readily offer their assent. Certainly it is a commitment that most evangelicals and Catholics share, at least in the abstract. It rings true to Christian theological and ethical convictions. It gives voice to high dimensions of Christian mysticism and piety. It points to God as the source of human worth and to God's command as the ultimate reason why human beings should think of one another in this exalted way.

If so, there is every reason for Christians, in our internal moral de-liberations and in our moral formation and discipling efforts, to seek to

5. This is my own definition, found in chapter 1 of *Sacredness of Human Life*.

imprint this vision on our own faith communities. We can, should, and often do preach, teach, and train believers in a vision along these lines. And where that vision takes root it often leads to a deepening and improving of interpersonal relations and enhanced Christian engagement with efforts to protect human beings from harm and contribute to their full flourishing.

WHAT RANGE OF ISSUES THIS
PURPORTED SACREDNESS MIGHT COVER

It should be immediately apparent that the understanding of life's sacredness presented here is comprehensive and holistic. It applies to each and every human being without exception and in all circumstances. Those taking this conviction seriously would be moved to ask such questions as: which types or groups of human beings are we not treating with proper reverence? What people on the planet most often find their lives cut short by violence? Who is being desecrated right now? What groups need help moving from mere survival to full-fledged flourishing?

My research provided confirmation that at least for the earliest Christians, these kinds of questions drew the church into holistic efforts to love and respect every human being and group that they encountered. It also led them to teach one another to abstain from a wide range of socially accepted practices that violated this standard. This included attending gladiator games, participating in capital punishment or war, abandoning their children, or allowing the sick to suffer and die alone. Christians became noteworthy for their expansive and inclusive love and care for the last, the least, and the lost, not only for their own suffering members but for those outside the Christian community. Christians cared about aborted babies, abandoned infants, starving children, terrorized wives, imprisoned enemies, shipwreck victims, tortured prisoners, dying elderly, bludgeoned soldiers, anyone in need. They also sought to create the kind of communities that overcame racial, ethnic, and national divisions.[6]

What range of issues is meant when Christians say they care about the sacredness of human life? A Christianity faithful to its most ancient heritage would have to answer: every issue implicating human survival and flourishing. Every individual or group at risk of having their lives desecrated would fall within the range of our concern.

6. Ibid., ch. 4.

But today, "sanctity of life" is most often used by American Christians as a slogan intended to communicate opposition to abortion. Sometimes that concern is extended to include embryonic life, as in some forms of stem cell research. Other times it includes worries over the end of life, as in resisting euthanasia. In other words, a conviction that is holistic and universal in principle, and in the earliest Christian practice, has become fixated on issues at the beginning and ending of life. Often this fixation has involved neglect of sacredness-of-life concerns that do not arise in hospital beds or abortion clinics, such as ecological disaster, war, and hunger. This is just bad Christian ethics, and it is unfortunate that it is this truncated ethic Christians most often bring into the public square. That demands the following question:

WHETHER THE SACREDNESS-OF-LIFE
IS A LEGITIMATE PUBLIC ETHIC

As I have presented it above, the conviction that human life is sacred and must be treated as such is a particularistic Christian theological-ethical belief. We (Christians) know this conviction is truthful based on divine revelation in Scripture and in Christ. Sacredness is an element of Christian tradition and historic moral practice. It is not a conviction accessible to mere human reason.

Our Catholic brethren, and some evangelical Protestants, might object at this point. They might argue that the sacred worth of the human person and the obligation to refrain from harming one another is indeed accessible even to fallen human reason. Anyone can know, at least, that wanton harm inflicted on one person by another is wrong and must be punished. There are laws against such violence in all kinds of cultures.

My response is to say that fallen human beings still *sometimes* demonstrate that they have epistemological access to the most minimal elements of the sacredness-of-life ethic, apart from biblical revelation. But my review of human history leaves me more impressed with both how minimal is this shared understanding, and how often even that moral minimum has been violated in the name of all kinds of ideologies. Everyone knows that murder is wrong, but that didn't stop Hitler, Stalin, Mao, Pol Pot, and Milosevic from murdering millions.

To be quite clear, I am saying that my study of the career of the sacredness-of-life idea has left me less rather than more convinced that it is universally accessible to fallen human reason. I believe instead that it is an aspect of special revelation and that the tradition of thought that has grown up in Christianity (and Judaism) around the concept is peculiar to our religious traditions. It is clear that through 1,500 years of Christendom these ideas penetrated cultures, like every other Christian idea did. But this does not mean that the sacredness of life is a truth accessible to unaided human reason.

Thus when contemporary American Christians invoke the sacredness of life to buttress, warrant, or attempt to settle public policy arguments in contemporary American life, we should be aware that we are importing into a secular/post-Christian/postmodern intellectual climate a major theological-ethical piece of our particular Christian tradition. We could once have perhaps expected that a broadly Christian cultural ethos would help our claims to seem persuasive even to those not committed to Christ. But it is now clear that sacredness of life language and its theological underpinnings are foreign to many in our culture. Others know exactly what "sacredness" means but simply do not share either the theological or the moral convictions involved.

This means that if we want to be heard in public discourse, and possibly even seek to have our vision make progress in law and culture, we will normally have to give public reasons for our beliefs. Many Christians understand this now, and often the language of "human dignity" is deployed. My own study leads me to the conclusion that though dignity language has come to be employed quite widely today in legal and moral philosophy, and sometimes even by Christians, its meaning is relatively unclear. In many ways it seems a stand-in for deeper religious claims viewed as too particularistic to be useful in public conversation.

If we instead insist on using "thick" Christian religious vocabulary like the sacredness of life in public and without any translation, we risk being misunderstood as attempting to impose our religious beliefs inappropriately on a diverse, pluralistic, separationist political community. With a declining but still robust share of the public with us, we might win occasional battles or at least prevent further losses, simply on the strength of our religious market share, but this seems neither an effective nor an appropriate strategy in the long run.

It is especially clear that reducing "sacredness of life" to issues at the edges of life is neither good theological ethics nor good public witness. I have already indicated why I don't think it is good theological ethics. I don't think it is good public witness because it fixates on the most debatable dimensions of a sacredness of life ethic, and because it violates what appears to be an intuitive human sensitivity to moral myopia, e.g.: "These Christians only seem to care about life before it is born and when it is ending, and nowhere in between." Our public witness has much more credibility when it is holistic and comprehensive, not to mention kind and compassionate. This leads to the following question:

WHETHER SPEAKING ABOUT SACREDNESS OF LIFE IS HELPFUL TO CHRISTIAN MISSION

By Christian mission here I speak of the broader Christian project of sharing the good news of Christ in the culture and in the world. It is clear, in part through the recent rise of aggressive anti-Christian secularism, that some of our public engagement has done more harm than good. Our aggressive pursuit of our public policy goals has inflamed opposition to Christianity and rejection of Jesus Christ. I am enough of a traditional evangelical to believe that public ethics is penultimate while the gospel is ultimate; thus negative impact on mission is a trade-off I am not willing to make.

This does not mean we must trim our sails entirely or simply withdraw from public articulation of a sacredness of life ethic. Such engagement can actually serve the broader work of Christian evangelism and mission if our ethics is holistic rather than focused only on the edges of life. If our tone is winsome, if we are compassionate toward, for example, women facing crisis pregnancies, if our witness reflects the complexity of the issues facing people, if we find ways to offer practical help that treats all people as sacred, we do well for both public ethics and Christian mission. But if we get sucked into the partisan vortex, and the partisan style of rancorous speech, and attacks on those who do not see it our way, and single-issue ethics, and spiraling extremism fueled by incomprehension of other views, we will indeed (continue to) harm our Christian witness in culture.

WHERE WE GO FROM HERE

I believe we can and should do the following things to advance public witness about the sacredness of life, and that evangelicals and Catholics can do much of this together:

1) We must constantly offer a holistic sacredness of life ethic, surprising those who expect narrow single-issue politics. This will require constant efforts to resist the centrifugal forces moving instinctive liberals narrowly left and instinctive conservatives narrowly right.

2) We must practice honoring life's sacredness through all kinds of service to the poor, those facing crisis pregnancies, the ill, the dying, the undereducated child, the abused, and so on. This is good Christian ethics that is respected by non-Christians too.

3) We must speak to and about those who differ with us as if their lives are sacred in God's sight as well, because they are.

4) When speaking of abortion, we must always communicate compassionate love for both mother and child. We must love both well to love either well.

5) We must look for common ground with those on the other side of abortion law and politics, and always keep lines of communication open.

6) We must look for incremental policy steps that reflect moral anxieties about abortion in the broader public, rather than absolutist strategies pleasing only to fellow true believers. These reachable incremental goals include matters such as waiting periods, parental consent, late-term abortions, abortions without mitigating circumstances such as rape and incest, etc.

7) Every step we take to make abortion harder to obtain should be matched by support for private and governmental measures that provide economic, emotional, and healthcare support for women and the babies they are shepherding into the world, perhaps against their will if laws are tightened.

WHETHER WE WILL "WIN"

It may be that we as evangelicals and Catholics seeking the common good together still will not "win" this struggle against abortion. It may be that, on abortion, our society is too far gone, too accustomed after forty years to underwriting the sexual revolution through routine abortion. It may be that our sentimental but in many ways hard-hearted culture will never be brought around to honoring life's full sacredness at any stage. If economic stagnation and decline continue, it may be that such pressures will continue to diminish human flourishing across the life span in our country.

We do not know what will happen in the future or whether Christian public witness will be effective. But we do know that we are always called to love God and love our neighbors. We are always called to be God's faithful people and to share the good news of Christ. We are always called to seek the good of our communities. It's not about winning. It's about faithful Christian witness.

10

Theological Perspectives on Nuclear Disarmament and Development

DREW CHRISTIANSEN, SJ

PART I

THE THEOLOGY OF PEACE
AND THE ETHICS OF DETERRENCE

IN A SERIES OF statements and actions anticipating the Nonproliferation Treaty Review in the spring of 2015, the Holy See (the Vatican) set its sights on nuclear abolition. In doing so, Archbishop Dominique Mamberti, the Holy See's Secretary for Relations with States, told the General Assembly of the International Atomic Energy Agency (IAEA), "The Holy See shares the thoughts and sentiments of most men and women of good will who aspire to a total elimination of nuclear weapons."[1]

In its diplomatic representations, the Holy See has upped the ante, asserting that the conditional acceptance of nuclear deterrence, articulated by the US bishops in their 1983 Pastoral Letter, "The Challenge of Peace," a lodestone for many ethicists and just war analysts, both Catholic and non-Catholic, no longer holds. Before the UN General Assembly in

---

1. Statement to the General Assembly of the IAEA, September 16, 2013.

2013, Archbishop Mamberti declared that the justification of deterrence formulated during the Cold War is "no longer tenable."[2] The archbishop argued, "We cannot justify the continuation of a permanent nuclear deterrence policy, given the loss of human, financial and material resources in time of scarcity of funds for health, education and social services around the world . . ."[3] The sacrifice of development to security must be ended.

The conditions set by "The Challenge of Peace" were: the possession of nuclear weapons *solely for deterrence* of nuclear attack by others, *sufficiency to deter* (i.e., an arsenal sufficient to deter but no larger), and, decisively, *progress toward disarmament*. While since the height of the Cold War there has been significant reduction in nuclear arsenals of the superpowers, the numbers of weapons held by the two sides still exceeds any reasonable standard of sufficiency to deter. Public authorities have at times explored and embraced various non-nuclear-deterrent purposes for nuclear arsenals, leaving ambiguity about their intended uses; and thirty years after "The Challenge of Peace" the world is still far from nuclear disarmament and the risks of proliferation are growing.

The "strict conditions" justifying deterrence have not been satisfied. The time when deterrence may have been reasonably tolerated in an attempt to forestall all-out nuclear war has passed. Neither the tests of conditionality, nor that of provisionality, have been met.[4] It is time for deterrence as an interim ethic to come to an end.

The Holy See has gone so far as to assert that deterrence, and implicitly the moral defense of its legitimacy, is an obstacle to nuclear disarmament. The prolongation of doctrines of deterrence, Archbishop Mamberti declared before the General Assembly "is driving the development of ever newer nuclear weapons arms thus preventing genuine nuclear disarmament."[5]

Advocates of deterrence, by contrast, argue that nuclear disarmament itself will require an assured deterrence, and the closer the world gets to

2. Address to the United Nations General Assembly, September 27, 2013.

3. Ibid.

4. On the conditions legitimating deterrence, see National Conference of Catholic Bishops, "The Challenge of Peace: God's Promise and Our Response" (USCC, 1983), no. 188. The provisional nature of the moral warrant for deterrence is found in the requirement that possession of nuclear weapons for deterrence must be accompanied by progress toward disarmament and in the pastoral letter's repeated profession that the unsatisfactory "peace of a sort" provided by deterrence by a constructive, "positive" peace delineated in Catholic Social Teaching. See especially nos. 200–1.

5. Ibid.

"Global Zero," the more, they are convinced, it will need a secure deterrent. Furthermore, they judge that the deterioration of Russian-US relations, the apparent violation of existing disarmament agreements, and the upgrading of weapons and delivery systems offers further reasons to resist calls to disarmament and make a more compelling moral as well as a strategic case for deterrence.

For my part, faced with what the US bishops once called "a folly that does not provide the security it promises," I believe we are challenged to replace "the peace of a sort" that we have tolerated for six decades with a genuine non-nuclear peace, where development becomes in the phrase of William James, "the moral equivalent of war." This alternative was advanced by Pope John Paul II in *Centesimus Annus*, when after contemplating the horror of war, he called for "a concerted worldwide effort in promoting development."[6] His program, of course, was anticipated by Paul VI's famous maxim, "Development is the new name for peace," and worked out in detail for our time by Pope Emeritus Benedict XVI in *Caritas in Veritate*.[7]

In his address to the UN General Assembly in September 2014, Cardinal Pietro Parolin (the Holy See's Secretary of State), citing the Holy Father's address of May 9 to top UN administrators, reiterated support for the UN's efforts "to ensure world peace, respect for human dignity, the protection of persons, especially the poorest and most vulnerable, and harmonious economic and social development."[8] He insisted that the UN and its member states have "an urgent and grave responsibility for the poor and excluded, mindful always that social and economic justice is an essential condition for peace."[9] Today no less than in 1968 when *Populorum Progressio* was released, development, especially for the poorest, is an essential component of peace.[10]

---

6. *Centesimus Annus*, no. 51.

7. See Pope Paul VI, "The Development of Peoples," nos. 76–80, and Benedict XVI, *Caritas in Veritate*," *passim* and especially nos. 71–72.

8. Parolin, Address to the United Nations General Assembly, September 30, 2014.

9. Ibid.

10. The linkage of development to peace has been a consistent theme of recent Catholic Social Teaching. In addition to *Populorum Progressio* and *Caritas in Veritate*, see Pope John Paul II, *Sollicitudo Rei Socialis*, especially no. 27. Nos. 22 and 23, moreover, interpreted the two blocs in the cold war as an obstacle to development. It (no. 23) also argued that the loss of resource to development through investment in arms production ought to be overcome.

PEACE THEOLOGY AND THE JUST WAR

The doctrine of nuclear deterrence, which blocks the path to global human development, relies on the historic role of the Just War Tradition in Catholic thought, the Church's pastoral practice, and Catholics' role in public deliberation on military policy. But once generated, just war thinking seldom recalls its theological foundations as a way of assessing whether it is accomplishing its proper end—the attainment of peace in the spirit of peace. "Even in waging war," Augustine counseled, "cherish the spirit of a peacemaker..."[11] Indeed, both the Scholastics and "the magisterial reformers" insisted that a Christlike will to peace is integral to the exercise of just war. When casuistry forgets this theological ground and becomes detached from the gospel message, it risks losing its sensitivity to the horrors of war, even nuclear war.

The intellectual invention by which Augustine made possible the shift in Latin Christianity from pacifism to just war was what historians of ethics call "the ethic of intention." That is, Augustine counseled that it is not the very real harms of war—the deaths, the wounds, the destruction—that matter but rather the spiritual evils motivating aggressors, in his words: "the love of violence, revengeful cruelty, fierce and implacable enmity, wild resistance and the lust for power."[12] So, the evils one had to avoid were not the physical, but the spiritual ones, and so all the just warrior had to do to be just was hold to a will to peace free of those spiritual evils. As long as one did not will these spiritual evils, one could wage war without guilt. The intention of restoring peace, by force when necessary, justified any physical evil that might be done.

Today we take the physical consequence of war, especially the consequences of nuclear war, more seriously. In a repudiation of war in *Centesimus Annus*, Pope John Paul offered a consequentialist critique of war. "No, never again war," he wrote,

> which destroys the lives of innocent people, teaches us how to kill, throws into upheaval even the lives of the people who do the killing and leaves behind a trail of resentment and hatred, thus

11. Augustine, Letter XLXXXIX.4, in Henry Paolucci, ed., *Saint Augustine: The Political Writings* (Washington, DC: Regnery, 1962).

12. Augustine, "Reply to Faustus the Manichean, 22," in Arthur F. Holmes, ed., *War and Christian Ethics* (Grand Rapids: Baker, 1975), 64.

making it all the more difficult to find a just solution of the very problem which provoked the war.[13]

John Paul's critique of war looks to consequences, spiritual and psychological consequences, but physical consequences as well. Accordingly, a right intention, what I prefer to call the will to peace, involves emphatically reducing the risks of war. It is no longer a matter of Catholic teaching holding a presumption against the use of force. It is rather demanding a conscious commitment to reduce the possible consequences of war, beginning with the reduction and elimination of nuclear weapons. Still, disarmament is only one element in the architecture of peace.

PART II

REQUIREMENTS OF PEACE
IN CONTEMPORARY CHURCH TEACHING

In assessing the will to peace in our current geopolitical context, a right intention refers to more than limits on the range of action open to warriors and war-planners. Rather, it should refer to the principles of a positive peace, articulated in *Pacem in Terris* and *Gaudium et Spes* as well as the annual papal Messages for the World Day of Peace.[14] Furthermore, it demands more than assessing war-planning in relation to those larger goals. Rather, it requires evaluation of states' overall geopolitical strategies in light of those teachings.

The Catholic vision of peace, found in the writings of Pope John XXIII and the Second Vatican Council and the unfolding of those theological motifs in papal teaching and Vatican diplomacy, includes: (1) progress toward

---

13. *Centesimus Annus*, no. 51. Contrast with Augustine, for whom the real evils in war are: the love of violence, the bloodlust, and the *libido dominandi* (the lust for rule). See *Contra Faustum*, 22.74.

14. Papal Messages for the World Day of Peace may be found in a variety of collections including *"Ways of Peace" Papal Messages for the World Days of Peace (1968–1986)* (Vatican City: Vatican, 1986). Chapter 6, "The Right to Peace," in André Dupuy, ed., *Pope John Paul II and the Challenges of Papal Diplomacy, Anthology (1978–2003)* (New York: Path to Peace Foundation, 2004). The Vatican Web site now organizes the messages solely by pontificate. Thus, for example, for Pope Francis, see http://w2.vatican.va/content/francesco/en/messages/peace/index.html.

disarmament, (2) strengthening the structures of global governance, (3) further promotion of development, and (4) protecting the integrity of creation.[15]

Thus, for example, the Church has been critical of the renewal and upgrade of nuclear weapons as contrary to the goal of disarmament. It, likewise, sees the expenditures on new weapons, as *Gaudium et Spes* declared, an illegitimate burden on humanity:

> While extravagant sums are being spent for the furnishing of ever new weapons, an adequate remedy cannot be provided for the multiple miseries afflicting the whole modern world. . . . New approaches initiated by reformed attitudes must be adopted to remove this trap and to restore genuine peace by emancipating the world from its crushing anxiety.[16]

The failure to make further significant progress toward nuclear disarmament even as contributions to development decline requires both a resetting of political priorities and a reallocation of resources. Recalibration of peace policy is the goal to which the Church needs to direct its social pastoral strategy.

Strengthening Global Governance

The Church is realistic. It understands that without a sufficiently robust set of global institutions, states will have to rely on themselves and on coalitions with other states to preserve world order. Fifty years ago in *Pacem in Terris* ("Peace on Earth"), the charter of Catholic political theology, Pope John XXIII, called for a public authority with the means "to operate in an effective manner on a worldwide basis."[17] Pope Emeritus Benedict, in *Caritas in Veritate*, noted in the same spirit that "In the face of the unrelenting growth of global interdependence, there is a strongly felt need, even in the midst of a global recession, for a reform of the *United Nations Organization*,

15. For reasons of space, I will discuss only the first three of these conditions of peace here. It will be easier to reflect on the requirements of the integrity of creation next year with the appearance of Pope Francis's anticipated encyclical on ecology.

16. Second Vatican Council, *Gaudium et Spes* (Pastoral Constitution on the Church in the Modern World), no. 81.

17. *Pacem in Terris*, nos. 136–37.

and likewise of *economic institutions and international finance,* so that the concept of the family of nations can acquire real teeth."[18] He explained,

> To manage the global economy; to revive economies hit by the crisis; to avoid any deterioration of the present crisis and the greater imbalances that would result; to bring about integral and timely disarmament, food security and peace; to guarantee the protection of the environment and to regulate migration: for all this, there is urgent need of a true world political authority" (italics in the original).

While the pope emeritus noted the need to implement such a global political authority "in solidarity and in a stratified way," all the same he insisted on the need of a global political authority "*to steer the globalization of humanity in relational terms, in terms of communion and the sharing of goods.*"[19]

A strengthening of global governance is also needed for the enforcement of peace. In his address to the General Assembly, mindful of the crisis in Syria and Iraq, Cardinal Parolin accented the need to study "the mechanisms used by the United Nations to prevent war, stop aggression, protect populations and help victims."[20] Again, referring to the crisis precipitated by the Islamic State, he said, "This reality requires a renewed United Nations that undertakes to foster and preserve peace."[21] While emphasizing the need to act within international law and utilize existing mechanisms, he urged that governments "[remain] open to the implications of the present moment." He concluded, "Such a willingness [to serve humanity on a multilateral basis], when concretely expressed in new juridical formulations, will certainly bring fresh vitality to the United Nations."[22] In short, the means currently available for keeping and securing the peace are too weak, and the international community needs to devise new tools, build them into international law, and support them with adequate personnel and funding.

---

18. *Caritas in Veritate*, no. 67.

19. Ibid., nos. 57 and 67. For further discussion of the global authority with respect to financial institutions, see Pontifical Council for Justice and Peace, "Towards Reforming the International Financial and Monetary Systems in the Context of Global Public Authority" (Vatican, 2011), with special emphasis on stratified solidarity (especially part 3, "An Authority Over Globalization").

20. See n. 8 above.

21. Ibid.

22. Ibid.

Renewed Commitment to Development

Beyond disarmament and the advancement of global governance, the path to peace must expand the reach of human development. The Ebola crisis demonstrated how far many poor countries still have to go in providing the basics of development in terms of establishing the necessary infrastructure of health. The gross deficiencies in that field demonstrate how weak international commitment is toward post-conflict reconstruction. The campaigns against the big three killers, tuberculosis, malaria, and HIV/AIDS have made great strides, but they have contributed as well to neglect of basic health needs: hospital beds, hydration units, even steady electrical supplies.

The reprioritizing of the global agenda from war and policing, beginning with nuclear disarmament, to the fundamentals of healthcare would go a long way towards providing increased physical security and improved quality of life in the neglected poor areas of the world. The "concerted worldwide campaign for development" John Paul II called for twenty years ago will be an investment in the long-term welfare of humanity.

The Catholic vision of development still rests, as both John Paul II in *Sollicitudo Rei Socialis* and Benedict XVI in *Caritas in Veritate* showed, on Paul VI's *Populorum Progressio*. The agenda of that encyclical is still valid today: aid, trade, and universal charity.[23] There is a new opportunity to refocus international aid in the assessment and re-formulation of the Millennial Development Goals in the 70th General Assembly. At the same time, obstacles to multilateral aid, like conditionality on contributions to the International Monetary Fund (IMF), must be found. In the field of trade, the agenda is the same as it was in 1968: equity for the poor countries, especially in the openness of developed countries to finished products from the developing world and in greater voice in trade bodies like the World Trade Organization.

Finally, a worldwide campaign for development, as John Paul II understood, can be the moral equivalent of war. It is time for young people in other fields, especially those trained in new technologies, to join the volunteers of Médecins Sans Frontières in service to the developing world. In the past quarter century, there has been a great growth in the new humanitarianism. The time is here to add to the numbers of the new humanitarians, so that even as we work to meet the enormous needs of people in

23. See *Populorum Progressio*, nos. 43–75.

complex emergencies and post-war reconstruction, we can work with the world's poorest to build a better, brighter life. The coming years are a time for genuine expressions of universal charity and generosity among nations in the cause of global human development.

PART THREE

The Common Good as Common Ground

11

Catholic and Evangelical Support for the Common Good and Human Rights

GLEN HAROLD STASSEN

IN OUR TIME OF harsh political polarization and partisanship over issues of economic justice, traditional church teaching on the Christian calling to support the common good of all persons offers us a breath of fresh air and clear moral guidance. The common good is central to Catholic social teaching, and more developed there than in evangelical teaching. So first I will analyze teaching on the common good in papal encyclicals, briefly, showing that it has at least eight connotations. Evangelicals are increasingly advocating the common good, but can develop a richer and more accurate sense of its meaning by learning from Catholic teaching.

EIGHT DIMENSIONS
OF THE MEANING OF THE COMMON GOOD

1. From individual interests to needs of the community, or the good of all people, all classes, and of each individual.[1]

In *Pacem in Terris* (Peace on Earth), § 52 and 53, Pope John XXIII writes that individuals "must bring their own interests into harmony with

---

1. Chris Korzen and Alexia Kelley, *A Nation for All: How the Catholic Vision of the Common Good Can Save America from the Politics of Division* (San Francisco: Jossey-Bass, 2008), xxi, 4–18.

the needs of the community." Our world is growingly interconnected, and therefore our responsibilities are also growingly interconnected. Those who wield power in government must act so as to advance the common good— of the whole community.

Throughout the encyclicals, the common good is contrasted with the kind of individualism in which people focus only on their own interests. Evangelicals can find a solid church tradition here to correct the ideology of libertarian individualism that has infiltrated and distorted some evangelical understanding of biblical teaching about God's caring for justice that restores just community. Some social scientists are seeing many young adult evangelicals working to correct that libertarianism.[2] These young evangelicals may be echoing, or stimulating, evangelical ethicists who are increasingly adopting Catholic teaching on the common good.

Benedict XVI's *Deus Caritas Est* (*God is Love*) makes this point in biblical terms:

> The awareness of this responsibility has had a constitutive relevance in the Church from the beginning: "All who believed were together and had all things in common; and they sold their possessions and goods and distributed them to all, as any had need" (Acts 2:44–5). In these words, Saint Luke provides a kind of definition of the Church, whose constitutive elements include fidelity to the "teaching of the Apostles," "communion" (koinonia), "the breaking of the bread," and "prayer" (cf. Acts 2:42).

The history of Catholic encyclicals for over one hundred years, from *Rerum Novarum* to the present, has included an affirmation of private property and a criticism of Marxist socialism, balanced by criticisms of selfish and greedy dimensions of capitalist individualism. God is the owner of the earth and property, and human "owners" are stewards, called to use the earth for the good of others, not merely themselves.[3]

2. See Brian Steensland and Philip Goff, *The New Evangelical Social Engagement* (New York: Oxford University Press, 2013).

3. In *Centesimus Annus*, Pope John Paul II writes:
Rerum novarum is opposed to state control of the means of production, which would reduce every citizen to being a "cog" in the state machine. It is no less forceful in criticizing a concept of the state which completely excludes the economic sector from the state's range of interest and action. There is certainly a legitimate sphere of autonomy in economic life which the state should not enter. The state, however, has the task of determining the juridical framework within which economic affairs are to be conducted, and thus of safeguarding the prerequisites of a free economy, which presumes a certain equality between the parties,

The papal encyclical *Rerum Novarum* says, "Civil society exists for the common good, and, therefore, is concerned with the interests of all in general, and with the individual interests in their due place and proportion" (§ 37). "Since it is intimately bound up with human nature, [it] cannot exist fully and completely unless the human person is taken into consideration. . . . All members of the state are entitled to share in it, although in different ways according to each one's tasks, merits and circumstances. . . . Without preference for any single citizen or civic group." The common good is referred to twenty times in Pope John XXIII's *Mater et Magistra*, and forty-seven times in his *Pacem in Terris*, often as "the common good of all" and the "universal common good" of all persons (§ 48 and 132–40). Its clear meaning for social justice is seen in the US Catholic Bishops' *Economic Justice for All*, which cites "common good" thirty-four times.

The encyclicals refer to humankind as our relatives, "the whole human family" (*Pacem in Terris*, § 132, *Gaudium et Spes* [*Joy and Hope*, also called the *Pastoral Constitution on the Church in the Modern World*], §§ 2, 3). "All people are created in the image of God, who 'from one ancestor has created the whole human race and made them live all over the face of the earth'" (Acts 17:26), as *Gaudium et Spes* § 24 says. This calls forth our loyalty to the whole human family, all created in the image of God, all loved by God, and so to be loved by all who love God.

2. The common good touches a) the whole person, the needs both of body and soul, both the material and the spiritual welfare of all citizens, b) with special attention to less fortunate persons, including immigrants and political refugees, and c) underdeveloped countries, globally (*Pacem in Terris* §§ 55–59, 103–8, and 121–5).[4] *Gaudium et Spes* emphasizes a special obligation to make ourselves neighbors to abandoned elderly persons,

---

such that one party would not be so powerful as practically to reduce the other to subservience. . . .

The state must contribute to the achievement of these goals both directly and indirectly. Indirectly and according to the principle of subsidiarity by creating favorable conditions for the free exercise of economic activity, which will lead to abundant opportunities for employment and sources of wealth. Directly and according to the principle of solidarity, by defending the weakest, by placing certain limits on the autonomy of the parties who determine working conditions, and by ensuring in every case the necessary minimum support for the unemployed worker.

4. See also David Hollenbach, *The Common Good and Christian Ethics* (New York: Cambridge University, 2002), 93 *et passim*.

underpaid foreign laborers, refugees, children who suffer, and hungry persons, quoting Matthew 25:40—"Just as you did it to one of the least of these who are members of my family, you did it to me." *Mater et Magistra* (§20, 78–80, 139) associates the common good with economic rights of all citizens, especially the weaker—workers, women, and children. It "must have as its fundamental objective... the rights of the human person."

Evangelicals want to base our ethics on biblical teaching, and especially the teaching of Jesus. We can appreciate Pope Benedict XVI's similar emphasis in his encyclical *Deus Caritas Est*: In Christ's parable of the Compassionate Samaritan, "Anyone who needs me, and whom I can help, is my neighbor. . . . Jesus identifies himself with those in need, with the hungry, the thirsty, the stranger, the naked, the sick and those in prison. 'As you did it to one of the least of these my brethren, you did it to me' (Matt 25: 40)."

3. "The ethnic characteristics of the various human groups are to be respected as constituent elements of the common good" (*Pacem in Terris*, § 55). So the common good is not only about individuals, but also about the ethnic groups in which individuals have their community, their support, their empowerment. Many Catholic congregations may be clearer about this in practice than the previous history of papal teachings was. Many evangelicals are increasingly working on cross-ethnic inclusiveness, and we need to emphasize such practices yet more in our churches.

4. Attention to the powerless: "Considerations of justice and equity can at times demand that those involved in civil government give more attention to the less fortunate members of the community, since they are less able to defend their rights and to assert their legitimate claims" (*Pacem in Terris*).[5] Benedict XVI's *Deus Caritas Est* makes the same point, and bases it in Jesus' actions and teaching:

> In Christ, in the Compassionate Samaritan, "Anyone who needs me, and whom I can help, is my neighbour. The concept of "neighbour" is now universalized, yet it remains concrete. Despite being extended to all mankind, it is not reduced to a generic, abstract and undemanding expression of love, but calls for my own practical commitment here and now. . . . Jesus identifies himself with those in need, with the hungry, the thirsty, the stranger, the naked,

5. The evangelical *For the Health of the Nation* affirms this extensively and with some concreteness, 371–72, as does chapter 11 of Ronald Sider and Diane Knippers, eds., *Toward an Evangelical Public Policy* (Grand Rapids: Baker, 2005).

the sick and those in prison. "As you did it to one of the least of these my brethren, you did it to me" (Matt 25:40).

5. Attention to society, to civil society and just conditions, and to individual needs. Pope John refers to *Mater et Magistra:* "the common good of all 'embraces the sum total of those conditions of social living whereby men are enabled to achieve their own integral perfection more fully and more easily.'"[6] Civil society includes not only governmental policies of justice, but all of us pursuing the common good together.

I notice in public discourse more frequent references such as "we are all in this together," along with more frequent references to the common good. In our polarized and overly selfish-individualistic society, we may be learning our need for Catholic (and evangelical) teaching on the common good, so we can develop more cooperation in working together for the common good.

Many evangelicals have highlighted Romans 13:3–4, saying government rewards those who do good, and executes wrath on the wrongdoer. Some, influenced by laissez-faire ideology, emphasize only government's negative role of restraining wrongdoing, and slight government's positive responsibility for promoting the common good. But Romans 13:4 says the government "is God's servant for your good." Here in verse 4, Paul is saying, in effect, that Catholics are right; the government also has the creative calling to promote the common good.

6. Human Rights: Pope John XXIII develops Catholic tradition further, connecting the common good more explicitly and directly with human rights: "The common good is chiefly guaranteed when personal rights and duties are maintained. The chief concern of civil authorities must therefore be to ensure that these rights are acknowledged, respected, coordinated with other rights, defended and promoted, so that in this way each one may more easily carry out his duties. For 'to safeguard the inviolable rights of the human person, and to facilitate the fulfillment of his duties, should be the chief duty of every public authority.'"[7] "If any government does not acknowledge the rights of man or violates them, it not only fails in its duty, but its orders completely lack juridical force" (*Pacem in Terris,* § 60). "It is also demanded by the common good that civil authorities should make

6. Cf. *Gaudium et Spes* § 26.
7. Here quoting the Pentecost 1941 radio message of Pius XII.

earnest efforts to bring about a situation in which individual citizens can easily exercise their rights and fulfill their duties as well. For experience has taught us that, unless these authorities make suitable action with regard to economic, political and cultural matters, inequalities between the citizens tend to become more and more widespread . . ." § 63.

Gaudium et Spes § 26 speaks similarly: "There is a growing awareness of the exalted dignity proper to the human person, since he stands above all things, and his rights and duties are universal and inviolable. There must be made available to all men everything necessary for leading a life truly human, such as food, clothing, and shelter; the right to choose a state of life freely and to found a family; the right to education, to employment, to a good reputation, to respect, to appropriate information, to activity in accord with the upright norm of one's own conscience, to protection of privacy, and to rightful freedom in matters religious."

7. The common good requires governmental institutions strong enough to promote the common good in civil society. "Today the universal common good poses problems of worldwide dimensions, which cannot be adequately tackled or solved except by the efforts of public authority endowed with a wideness of powers, structure and means of the same proportions, that is, of public authority which is in a position to operate in an effective manner on a worldwide basis" (*Pacem in Terris,* § 137). "This public authority, having worldwide power and endowed with the proper means for the efficacious pursuit of its objective, which is the universal common good in its concrete form, must be set up by common accord and not imposed by force" (§ 138). "This public and universal authority, too, must have as its fundamental objective the recognition, respect, safeguarding and promotion of the rights of the human person" (§ 139). Here the principle of subsidiarity, that local matters are best handled by local authorities where they are adequate to the task, and matters that need wider government authority, are best handled by broader authorities, offers a helpful concept: "The worldwide public authority is not intended to limit the sphere of action of the public authority of the individual state, much less to take its place. On the contrary, *its purpose is to create, on a world basis, an environment in which the public authorities of each state, its citizens, and intermediate associations, can carry out their tasks,* fulfill their duties and exercise their rights with greater security" (§ 141, emphasis added). John XXIII commends the United Nations Organization and the

Universal Declaration of Human Rights (§§ 142–45; cf. *Gaudium et Spes*, § 33). Evangelical James Skillen, in *In Search of the Common Good*, 274–75, makes a parallel argument, as does the chapter on peace and war in *Toward an Evangelical Public Policy*.

8. We need to supplement this by saying the common good requires care for the creation, on which our common good depends. Earlier encyclicals as well as earlier evangelical statements, were less aware of our growing threat to the creation, but this awareness is rapidly growing among Catholics and evangelicals. Destroying the creation will result in a massive attack on the common good of everyone, especially the less powerful. Present focus on consuming more nonrenewable resources for our own comfort deprives next generations of those resources. Nonrenewable resources do not grow back. Jesus warned us pointedly about the destructiveness of greed.

CATHOLICS ADVOCATE
HUMAN RIGHTS FOR ALL PERSONS

We have already seen that the popes emphasize human rights as part of the common good. Both evangelicals and Catholics advocate human rights along with the common good, which can give them the right balance. During our consultations, John Borelli of Georgetown University wrote me what could have been my own words: "Some misunderstandings of the common good could so emphasize the collective good that they would neglect the rights of individuals and minorities, and some misunderstandings of human rights could so emphasize individual rights that they neglect the common good of the society. Therefore, we need to emphasize both the common good and human rights to correct both those misunderstandings." Emphasizing the common good makes clear that our shared advocacy of human rights is 1) not merely individualistic, and 2) does include obligation, duty, responsibility to aid the common good of others, and 3) especially focuses our attention on the less powerful whose rights are being violated. Thus the common good puts human rights in a more adequate context. And similarly, human rights prevent the common good from becoming collectivist and oppressive to individuals. So common good should be understood this way, as it is in Catholic encyclicals and in evangelical publications. Dan Finn also affirmed "distinguishing the Christian view of rights (as simultaneously entailing obligations)" from the "view of rights as claims only."

The other criticism of human rights from the O'Donovans is that they are based on Occam's nominalism. Nicholas Wolterstorff has refuted that in *Justice: Rights and Wrongs*, and I have refuted it in my 1992 book, *Just Peacemaking: Transforming Initiatives for Justice and Peace*. The first comprehensive doctrine of human rights was written by Baptist Richard Overton in the struggle for religious liberty and against the Thirty Years' War and other wars of religion, in the 1640s in England, and it was thoroughly biblically grounded, not secular. It is now based in revulsion against Nazism, as expressed in the Universal Declaration of Human Rights, in the US civil rights movement, in the struggle for women's rights, immigrant rights, and opposition against torture of defenseless prisoners.

Furthermore, as Gunnar Myrdal's study of American society, *An American Dilemma* (1941), argued, human rights are so strongly built into American identity that he called human rights "the American Creed." Unusually for a sociologist, he went out on a limb, predicting that the American creed of human rights would soon defeat racial segregation and segregation laws. He was basically predicting the civil rights movement and its victories twenty-five years in advance—because of the evidence he saw of a strong American tradition of human rights not for "self," but for persons oppressed. From the Declaration of Independence to the Constitution to Abraham Lincoln to Martin Luther King Jr., human rights are in American memory and American identity. They focus our attention on "liberty and justice for all," and especially on those less wealthy or less powerful who are being deprived of their human rights.

Of course, honesty requires that we admit we are a pluralistic society, with competing and less helpful traditions and ideologies that support racism, militarism, and individualistic greed. We won't succeed in persuading people to abandon these unhelpful ideologies unless we offer a better and more just tradition that has resonance in American identity. These and the tradition of human rights compete with each other. Human rights offer an identity-based tradition to help us work to correct other strains in American experience. But they need to be combined with the tradition of the common good, so they are not distorted into their opposite—possessive individualism of "my rights and let others fend for themselves."

Modern Catholic teaching on human rights begins with Pope Leo XIII, especially in *Rerum Novarum* (1891). Pope John XXIII's *Pacem in Terris*

(1963), and Vatican II's *Dignitatis Humanae,* signed by Paul VI, were major developments of a tradition that runs back through Thomas Aquinas, medieval Decretists, early church fathers, and the Bible.[8] Pope Leo especially argued for "the basic economic rights to food, clothing, shelter, organization, and a living wage" as essential ingredients in the right to life. Pius XI, Pius XII, especially John XXIII, Paul VI, and John Paul II emphasized three sets of rights—*basic needs, freedoms, and community relationships*—which must be protected for the life of every individual person. The popes also emphasized social and political institutions, structures, and duties that bind us together in supporting and defending human rights.

"Catholic rights theory is far removed from individualist or libertarian social philosophy. [It] is personalist, not individualist, and it recognizes that persons are essentially social and institution-building beings."[9] David Hollenbach's *Claims in Conflict* provides a schema identifying eight different sets of rights in *Pacem in Terris,* each with a personal, social, and instrumental claim. Based on Catholic social teaching, Hollenbach concludes that societies' efforts to implement human rights should prioritize the needs of the poor over the wants of the rich, the freedom of the dominated over the liberty of the powerful, and participation of marginalized groups over preserving an order that excludes them. It is important that we affirm human rights not only for individuals but also the group memberships and structures supporting rights.

Running through all these documents is the central theological affirmation that all persons are created in the image of God, and that we all have a duty to defend all persons' human dignity and human rights. This gives all persons rights and duties. It has a quadruple basis: natural law that can be understood by natural reason, Christian faith centering in biblical revelation of creation in the image of God, redemption by Jesus Christ who teaches that God gives sun and rain to the just and unjust alike, and eschatological hope for redemptive justice.

Vatican II took place in a time of increasing awareness and attention to the voices of Catholics from many different nations, and therefore honesty about the distortions, disagreements, and diversities of human reason in any one culture. Furthermore, Catholic biblical scholarship was growing

8. Wolterstorff, *Justice: Rights and Wrongs* (Princeton, NJ: Princeton University Press, 2008), and Hollenbach, *Claims in Conflict: Retrieving and Renewing the Catholic Human Rights Tradition* (Mahwah, NJ: Paulist, 1979).

9. Hollenbach, *Claims in Conflict,* 17–20, 49, 97–98, and 203–4.

in impressive insightfulness and in public attention. Hence the basis of human rights in biblical teaching and the usefulness of human rights for affirming and incorporating the perceptions and insights of Catholics and non-Catholics from diverse nations was becoming increasingly appreciated. Hence Vatican II saw human rights as a helpful articulation of what Catholic churches had long intended in their teaching of natural law.[10]

I write as a Baptist. Baptists have advocated the human right of religious liberty from our origin in the early 1600s, and by the 1640s this had developed into advocacy of a comprehensive threefold doctrine of human rights very similar to present-day Catholic teaching. I need to confess that in the mid-twentieth century many Baptists harbored some anti-Catholicism because of stories (true or false or exaggerated) about alleged Catholic opposition to religious liberty for Baptists in countries where Catholics dominated.

Therefore, I happily taught the Vatican II document on religious liberty in my large Baptist seminary. I would regularly ask my Baptist students if they found anything missing, or misstated, in the document on religious liberty. They could not find anything they would take issue with. Except one time one of the students said: "This part on religious liberty even for Muslims maybe goes too far"! (The original Baptists in the 1600s had championed religious liberty for Baptists and other Protestants, and for Catholics, Jews, and "Turks," by which they meant Muslims. My student needed Catholics to teach him his Baptist tradition.)

EVANGELICALS ARE INCREASINGLY ADVOCATING THE COMMON GOOD.

Toward an Evangelical Public Policy, edited by Ronald Sider and Diane Knippers, is an important recent statement of evangelical teaching on public ethics.[11] It balances more conservative and more progressive evangelical ethicists, and its advocacy on diverse issues is remarkably similar to the Catholic *Compendium of Social Doctrine of the Church*, published by the Vatican. In fact, our noticing the striking and extensive similarity between *TEPP* and the *Compendium* is what led Joseph Fahey and me initially to propose our present dialogue sessions of Catholics and Evangelicals for the Common Good. *Toward an Evangelical Public Policy* signals the increas-

10. Ibid., 113–14 and 124–133.

11. Sider and Knippers, eds., *Toward an Evangelical Public Policy*.

ing advocacy of the common good among leading evangelical ethicists. It advocates the term "common good" thirty-two times.

Toward and Evangelical Policy was then summarized in the brief document *For the Health of the Nation*, which was endorsed by all board members of the National Association of Evangelicals. This gives it the closest I can think of to Vatican approval among evangelicals, although admittedly nothing among us can come very close to that level of authority. Still, I am hoping it is a significant step in developing a tradition for us.

The phrase "common good" appears three times in the short summary, *For the Health of the Nation*. When Christians do justice as part of neighbor-love, "it can show those who are not believers how the Christian vision can contribute to the common good and help alleviate the ills of society." The section on "the structure of public life" states: "God has ordered human society with various institutions and set in place forms of government to maintain public order, to restrain human evil, and to promote the common good." The section on human rights states, "government must fulfill its responsibility to provide for the general welfare and promote the common good."

Beyond that, the document uses a series of terms virtually synonymous with the common good: "the *well-being of the entire world*"; God's "kingdom would be marked by *justice, peace, forgiveness, restoration, and healing for all*"; the church's calling "will require us to demonstrate God's love *for all*, by crossing racial, ethnic, economic, and national boundaries"; "We must practice humility and cooperation to achieve modest and attainable goals for *the good of society*." Immediately after affirming that the government's task is to "maintain public order, to restrain human evil, and to promote the common good," we read: "God has called *all people* to share responsibility for creating *a healthy society*." "We support the democratic process in part because people continue to be sufficiently blessed by God's common grace that they can seek not only their own betterment, but also *the welfare of others*." "God has blessed America with bounty and strength, but unless these blessing are used for *the good of all*, they will turn to our destruction." In the next sentence, the notion of "the good of all" is extended internationally: "We must also balance our natural affection for our country with a love for people of *all nations*. . . . Care for the vulnerable should extend *beyond our national borders*." On seeking justice and compassion for the poor and vulnerable, the booklet states: "By deed and parable, [Jesus] taught us that *anyone in need* is our neighbor . . . Because *all people* are created in the image of God, we owe each other help in time of need." Government's role is not "to provide everything that humans need for their *well-being*," but to "strengthen families, schools, businesses, hospitals, social-service organizations, and other institutions so that they can contribute to *human welfare*." The penultimate sentence of the entire document summarizes the main thrust of the argument: "We call all Christians to a renewed political engagement that aims to protect the vulnerable and poor, to guard the sanctity of human life, to further racial reconciliation and justice, to renew the family, to care for creation, and to promote justice, freedom, and peace *for all*."

In a 2007 essay for the Society of Christian Ethics, Jeffrey Greenman, then Associate Dean at Wheaton College, said the authors of

> *For the Health of the Nation*, the most prominent recent attempt within North American evangelicalism to develop a theological framework for public engagement . . . have adopted an account of the common good that is [strikingly similar to] official Catholic teaching, and are developing a theology of the common good drawing creatively on the biblical notion of *shalom. For the Health of the Nation* bears striking resemblance to the 2003 statement by the U.S. Roman Catholic bishops, *Faithful Citizenship.* . . . Each calls their respective community to deeper and more extensive public involvement. Each champions humility and civility. The evangelicals even appear to have adopted the characteristic tone and style of official Roman Catholic teaching documents. . . .
>
> The evangelical document . . . relies more directly on "what the Bible says" as the foundation for its claims. The NAE document assumes a conversionist piety. There are several references to the need for individuals to be "transformed" by personal faith in Christ. The USCCB statement assumes a sacramental piety, depicting the eucharist as the place where Catholics "find the direction and strength to take what we believe into the public square . . ."
>
> There is clear convergence of moral-social vision in these documents. . . . The seven principles promulgated by each document are nearly exact parallels. In the case of five specific principles—regarding human dignity, family, human rights, the poor, and care for creation—the language used is nearly interchangeable and the moral norms described are virtually identical. With regard to a sixth principle there is a merely semantic difference that conceals substantive agreement. The Roman Catholic document's reference to the principle of "solidarity with all humanity" is expounded exclusively in terms of "the pursuit of justice and

peace" and the Gospel's calling for Christians to be "peacemakers." This is exactly what the evangelical statement discusses under the principle that calls Christians to "seek peace and work to restrain violence."[12]

Greenman concludes: "What is striking is how much the evangelicals sound like Catholics." He sees only one topic where parallelism is lacking: "It is widely recognized that issues related to the right to work, the conditions of labor, a living and just wage, private property, strikes, workers' associations and other aspects of economic justice have held a prominent position in modern Catholic social teaching from its inception in the encyclical *Rerum Novarum*" (1891). . . . Although evangelicals typically have given relatively little sustained consideration to modern issues of economic justice, *For the Health of the Nation* does include a significant discussion under its principle of 'seeking justice and compassion for the poor and vulnerable.'"[13]

Greenman here writes perceptively. He says exactly what I would say. I quote him, a respected evangelical from perhaps the most respected evangelical college, to give added authority to what would otherwise be my words.

GROUNDING THE COMMON
GOOD IN A THICK TRINITARIANISM

Richard Mouw is the widely respected Reformed theological ethicist and president of the large, evangelical Fuller Theological Seminary. Jeffrey Greenman points out that in a chapter entitled "Seeking the Common Good," Mouw argues that "Christians must actively work for the well-being of the larger societies in which we have been providentially placed." He appeals to Jeremiah 29:7: "But seek the welfare (*shalom*) of the city where I have sent you into exile, and pray to the Lord on its behalf, for in its welfare (*shalom*) you will find your welfare (*shalom*)." Jeremiah 29:7 is also central for the leading Anabaptist theological ethicist, John Howard Yoder, as in his last book, *For the Nations*. So Jeremiah 29:7 is a key theological grounding for the common good, uniting two major wings of evangelical ethicists.

12. Jeffrey P. Greenman, "Toward an Evangelical Ethic of the Common Good: Pitfalls and Possibilities," essay presented at The Society of Christian Ethics, 48th Annual Meeting, Dallas, Texas, January, 2007.

13. Ibid.

It unites the creation-based Reformed argument and the Christ-based Anabaptist argument. Greenman writes:

> In a lecture in 2003, Mouw offers a broad analysis of the current strengths and weaknesses of evangelical Protestant social engagement. His main point in the lecture is that "evangelicals need to develop a theology of the common good." He suggests "Roman Catholicism has much to teach us here" and [commends] David Hollenbach's book, *The Common Good and Christian Ethics*, saying: "it's the kind of book that Evangelicals need to read and to struggle with and think about ways in which we might develop a very similar theological, philosophical understanding of the common good. I've been preaching this quite a bit." Mouw states that in thinking through the common good, "Biblically there's a lot we can draw on there." He returns to Jeremiah 29 and 1 Peter 2 in order to spell out that the common good is what the Old Testament prophets talked about as shalom.[14]

Mouw is focusing here on the question that can be fruitful for our work together, in common—how best to ground our theological arguments for the common good. *For the Health of the Nation* (355, 366) says: "As Christians committed to the full authority of Scripture, our normative vision must flow from the Bible and from the moral order that God has embedded in his creation." The Reformed tradition and papal teaching pay greater attention to the creation of all humankind in the image of God. Anabaptists, Baptists, and many in the free-church tradition pay greater attention to Jesus' teaching of love for all persons on whom God bestows rain and sunshine (Matthew 5:43–48). The will of God the Creator is revealed in Jesus Christ.

Thus *For the Health of the Nation* explains "the basis for Christian Civic Engagement" in two paragraphs, one emphasizing God as Creator and the other emphasizing Jesus Christ as Lord. Evangelicals want a stronger focus on Jesus' compassion demonstrated in his death on the cross: "This is how God showed his love among us: He sent his one and only Son into the world that we might live through him. This is love: not that we loved God, but that he loved us and sent his Son as an atoning sacrifice for our sins. Dear friends, since God so loved us, we also ought to love one another. No one has ever seen God; but if we love one another, God lives in us and his love is made complete in us'" (1 John 4:9–12).

14. Ibid.

And we need the Pentecostal theme that in the book of Acts of the Apostles, the Holy Spirit calls us not to limit the gospel to one nation, but to expand our love to the common good of all nations, from Jerusalem to the uttermost parts of the earth. And John 3:8—"The wind blows where it chooses, and you hear the sound of it, but you do not know where it comes from or where it goes. So it is with everyone who is born of the Spirit." The Holy Spirit cannot be contained by one nation or one in-group.

This completes our thick Trinitarian theological ethic, grounded in God the Creator, revealed in Jesus Christ, calling us to repentance for our ideological captivities and empowering us to live through the Holy Spirit. The challenge for evangelicals is to find the terms or loyalties within evangelical tradition and experience that can point people toward emphasizing the common good. Our evangelism emphasizes experience, both experience of conversion to accept Jesus Christ as Lord and Savior, and practical life experience. We need to emphasize that Jesus Christ acted out of love toward many people who were disregarded by their society—lepers, prostitutes, Samaritans, the disabled, the poor who were being treated unjustly, and even Roman soldiers, and that Jesus' traveling to Jerusalem to call the authorities there to repent and to practice justice for the poor was an act of love—which led to his crucifixion.

For the Health of the Nation also says " we must do detailed social, economic, historical, jurisprudential, and political analysis . . ." Thus David Hollenbach argues incisively that we won't solve problems of inner-city poverty or world hunger until we see others' children as children of our human family. We need churches to engage members in specific practices of serving the needs of diverse other people, as Pope Benedict XVI emphasizes in the second half of *Deus Caritas Est.* And these practices need to be accompanied with group discussions interpreting causes of poverty and remedies that affirm loyalty to the common good of all. I suggest our theology for the common good emphasize specific practices by church members and small-group discussion. We need more specific development of our ecclesiology.

Max Stackhouse distinguishes a continental form of Calvinism epitomized by Karl Barth, an imperial form of Calvinism epitomized by dogmatic fundamentalism, and a free-church Calvinism, epitomized by voluntary community and disciplined personal life.[15] The free-church

---

15. Stackhouse, *Creeds, Society and Human Rights: A Study in Three Cultures* (Grand Rapids: Eerdmans, 1984), 56–68.

Calvinism synthesizes the Calvinist tradition with more Christ-centered and Anabaptist strands. I advocate that we weave together arguments from creation of all in the image of God with arguments from Jesus' teachings on love and Jesus' love demonstrated in the cross, and the Holy Spirit as calling us to repent from limiting our caring to our in-group.

DEEPER UNDERSTANDING OF SIN
AS GROUNDING FOR THE COMMON GOOD

Evangelicals emphasize that Jesus Christ died *for our sin*. But we need a deeper doctrine of sin. Paul Freston—an evangelical Brazilian sociologist—has written *Evangelicals and Politics in Asia, Africa, and Latin America*. He shows that on the whole, we have not done well when we have attained political power. We have been willing to give our political support to a would-be ruler who promises to do special favors for our church or for Christian faith, and too unconcerned for justice for the society as a whole—in other words, for the common good. We have been too lax in supporting checks and balances for the concentrated power of an authoritarian ruler. We have been too inclined to believe that we are Christians, and therefore we and our Christian ruler, know what is right, and anyone who disagrees with us is on the side of evil. So we do not listen well to other perspectives. I suggest this stems from naiveté about the narrow interests of the would-be ruler, and from a view of sin that believes we have overcome it because we are converted to Christ.

Therefore we evangelicals need a more profound understanding of sin as we advocate the common good. I urge evangelicals and Catholics to ground the common good not only in advocacy of an ideal, but also in the need for checks and balances against narrow interests, including concentrated economic wealth and power.

"We know that since the Fall, people often abuse power for selfish purposes. As Lord Acton noted, power tends to corrupt and absolute power corrupts absolutely. Thus we thank God for a constitutional system that decentralizes power through the separation of powers, fair elections, limited terms of office, and division among national, state, and local authorities."[16]

Here I pick up a theme from Nicholas Wolterstorff:

16. *For the Health of the Nation*, 367.

> The Christian will never weary of insisting that the task of the state in God's creational and providential order is to promote justice and serve the common good. . . . The state often fails in its task of promoting justice by overlooking or refusing to acknowledge the occurrence of injustice. . . . Sometimes this happens because the state is in the grip of the ideology of private enterprise, the ideology of nationalism, whatever. Often it happens because the state is in the control of rich and powerful persons who see to it that they remain free to go about their unjust ways. In such situations it is the calling of the Christian to denounce the ideologies, bring the injustice to light, name it for what it is, namely injustice, and insist that the state not shirk its task.[17]

The encyclicals achieve clarity by criticizing a Marxist ideology of the left and a laissez-faire ideology of the right, before stating the church's common-good position. Sider does likewise in his chapter in *TEPP*. I suggest we make Ephesians 4:14-15 a theological theme: "Then we will no longer be infants, tossed back and forth by the waves, and blown here and there by every wind of teaching and by the cunning and craftiness of men in their deceitful scheming. Instead, speaking the truth in love, we will in all things grow up into him who is the Head, that is, Christ."

Reformed evangelical James Skillen urges that no one other than the Creator God may be acknowledged as the ultimate reference point of human authority and responsibility (Exod 20:1-11; Deut 5:1-15; 1 Cor 15:20-28).[18] This guards against authoritarian-tending thought that locates the common good in a political or economic authority, and also against a liberal-tending thought that bases political authority in the right of individuals and corporations against interference with their liberty. Crucial for Skillen is that the common good is a transcendent norm that rejects "an all-dissolving, omnicompetent, totalitarian norm." It "can be realized only through the simultaneous recognition and affirmation of a *diversity* of nonpolitical responsibilities in a *differentiated* society." He says Aquinas improves over Aristotle and Plato and Calvin carries differentiation still farther. I add: free-church Puritanism, influenced by the Anabaptist stream, insists on religious liberty and independence of diverse churches from the state as well as from a single ecclesiastical authority, thereby carrying differentiation yet farther.

17. Wolterstorff, in Sider and Knippers, eds., *Toward an Evangelical Public Policy*, 156-57.

18. Ibid., 260 and 256-57.

Menno Simons in the sixteenth century and Dietrich Bonhoeffer in the twentieth century insisted that Christ is Lord over the state as well as over the economy, the family, and the church. This parallels the Reformed insistence that the common good and human rights are based not merely in the liberal right of individuals against interference, but in the will of God the Creator.

GROUNDING THE COMMON GOOD IN JUSTICE FOR ALL

Most evangelicals are members of churches with congregational self-government. This gives us a natural tendency to adapt to the culture of our members, influenced by their social location. It may give us an advantage in appealing to prospective members from that social location, and a disadvantage in being "tossed one way and another and carried along by every wind" of ideology. The trick is to select those parts of the culture that are compatible with the way of Christ, when we seek to communicate the gospel in public discourse, and to reject those parts that advocate individualistic greed or are otherwise incompatible with the gospel. Perhaps we could make use of that part of the US Pledge of Allegiance that says "justice for all." Perhaps we could also speak as the Declaration of Independence does of human rights for all, given by our Creator. This will translate a core meaning of the common good in language that sounds familiar to evangelicals influenced by US culture. *For the Health of the Nation says:* "We believe it is our calling to help government live up to its divine mandate to render justice."

But we mean something different by justice than US culture usually does. Ronald Sider and Stephen Mott have done a masterful job spelling out what justice means with concrete content based primarily on interpretation of the Old Testament, and especially the prophets.[19]

EVANGELICAL TEACHING ON HUMAN RIGHTS SUPPORTS THE COMMON GOOD.

The resemblance of evangelical teaching on human rights to Catholic teaching is clear in *Toward an Evangelical Public Policy* and *For the Health*

19. See Sider's chapter in *Toward an Evangelical Public Policy*, which advocates the common good by name eight times.

of the Nation, which has extensive emphasis on creation of all persons in the image of God, and a comprehensive doctrine of human rights: "Because God created human beings in his image, all people share in the divine dignity" (hence sanctity of human life, opposition to abortion and euthanasia). "As recipients of God's gift of embodied life, people need food, nurture, shelter and care . . ." (Hence the *right to life* includes the right to these essential ingredients of an embodied life.) "Because all people are created in the image of God, we owe each other help in time of need" (therefore rights of justice for the poor and vulnerable). "Because God created human beings in his image, we are endowed with rights and responsibilities. In order to carry out these responsibilities, human beings need the *freedom* to form associations, formulate and express beliefs, and act on conscientiously held commitments. . . . Because the Creator gave human beings liberty, we believe that religious liberty" is crucial. (Because human dignity requires the *right to dignity in community*), God's design for human existence also implies a right to marry, enjoy family life, and raise and educate children, as well as the freedom to form associations.

The major denominations, Protestant and Catholic, have all adopted official statements advocating human rights for all persons. Running through these statements is a threefold definition of human rights, basically similar to the threefold definition in section II above and to the threefold evangelical emphasis in the previous paragraph. Therefore, let me summarize these simply for clarity:

1. The right to religious and civil liberty.

2. The right to life both in the sense of not being killed and in the sense of the right to ingredients needed for life—food, nurture, shelter, care, and education.

3. The right to dignity in community—family life, forming associations, religious community, citizenship in a state.

Almost the same three dimensions of human rights were advocated in 1647 by the first comprehensive doctrine of human rights. The full concept of human rights was first developed and articulated during the free-church struggle for the right of religious liberty in Puritan England in the 1640s, by the Anabaptist/Baptist Richard Overton.[20] Overton advocated human rights

20. Richard Tuck, *Natural Rights Theories: Their Origin and Development* (Cambridge: Cambridge University Press, 1979); William Haller, *Tracts on Liberty in the Puritan Revolution, 1638-1647*, vol. 1 (New York: Atheneum, 1969); Wolfgang Huber

in his satire, *The Arraignment of Mr. Persecution* (1645). His arguments are based on Scripture as authoritative: he shows an extensive knowledge of the New Testament, and the passages on which he focuses fit with his own confession of faith as early as 1615, when he joined the Waterlander Mennonite Church in Holland. He also argued from natural law as articulated by churches for centuries prior to the Puritan period. And he argued on the basis of historical experience seen from the perspective of his faith: religious persecution causes wars, divisions, bloodshed, and hypocrisy; most wars, and especially the Thirty Years' War that killed one-third of the people of Germany, were fought over which religion would dominate and exclude the other. The right to religious liberty would be a dramatic peacemaking initiative: there would be no need to fight a war to get "our" faith to control the government. (We are seeing this truth at the time of this writing, as the Assad government of Syria employs desperate violence against civilians because if the other side wins, it fears drastic persecution for itself and its adherents. Syria lacks a strong tradition of human rights, including religious liberty, for minorities who are not in power.) Overton was also motivated by biblical concern for justice for the poor, intensified when he got to know the poor who were jailed for their debts, as he was jailed for his faith.

His comprehensive doctrine of human rights as belonging to all persons, including Protestants, Catholics, Jews and Muslims, was born fully developed, comprehensive even by present-day standards, in "An Appeal . . . to the Free People" (1647). It included three major categories of rights: (1) *religious liberty and civil liberty*: freedom from coercion in religion, from governmental establishment of religion, and from taxation for religion; freedom of the press; the right of prisoners not to be starved, tortured, or extorted; the right not to be arbitrarily arrested nor forced to incriminate oneself; the right to speedy trial; the right to understand the law in one's own language; and equality before the law; (2) *basic needs and economic rights*: the right not to be imprisoned for debt; the right to trade internationally without restrictions by monopolies; the right to a free education for everyone; the right to housing and care for poor orphans, the widowed,

and Heinz Eduard Tödt, *Menschenrechte: Perspektiven einer menschlichen Welt* (Stuttgart: Kreuz Verlag, 1977); Glen Stassen, "The Christian Origin of Human Rights," in Stassen, *Just Peacemaking: Transforming Initiatives for Justice and Peace* (Louisville: Westminster John Knox, 1992); Michael Westmoreland White, "Setting the Record Straight: Christian Faith, Human Rights, and the Enlightenment," *Annual of the Society of Christian Ethics* (1995), 75–96.

the aged, and the handicapped; and the right of the poor to their portion of land; and (3) *rights of community participation* in choosing a government that is responsive to the people and the common good; the right to vote and participate in government regardless of one's beliefs; and the right to petition Parliament.

This third set of rights, human dignity in community participation, is important for evangelicals to remember. Evangelicals often tend to be individualistic. They rightly emphasize conversion, the individual adoption of faith by each person. This is a strength. But it can become myopic, neglecting the importance of community. Many evangelical statements of the human right to religious liberty affirm individual liberty and conscience, but forget to emphasize the human right to form a church community with its rights to shared worship and public expression of the faith. The Vatican II document on religious liberty adds the right to community expression of the faith in a way that evangelicals can learn from. And the papal encyclicals also emphasize social and political institutions, structures, and duties that bind us together in supporting and defending human rights.

Combining human rights with the common good makes clear that human rights are not merely individual assertion of "my rights and let others fend for themselves." Human rights focus our attention on those whose rights are being violated, not on "my rights." They are based on compassion, on love for the poor, the powerless, the dominated, the excluded, the victims of violence. They include *the obligation* to come to the aid of those deprived of their rights. The US civil rights movement, the struggle for women's rights, the struggle for religious liberty for minorities, the struggle against torture of defenseless prisoners, the struggle for comprehensive immigration reform that offers a path to citizenship, have not been merely a struggle for "my selfish rights," but a fulfillment of the biblical obligation to defend justice for the deprived—the widows, the orphans, the poor, and the immigrants (sojourners, aliens). God cares deeply for justice. Human rights for all opposes ideologies of greed that insist on hoarding wealth for the few without restraints on greed.

For the Health of the Nation also calls us to "Labor for the Health of Creation." It is saying that environmental protection is crucial for the human rights to life of present and future generations.

> Because clean air, pure water, and adequate resources are crucial
> to public health and civic order, government has an obligation
> to protect its citizens from the effects of environmental degrada-
> tion. This involves . . . the urgent need to relieve human suffering

caused by bad environmental practice. . . . We urge Christians to shape their personal lives in creation-friendly ways: practicing effective recycling, conserving resources, and experiencing the joy of contact with nature. We urge government to encourage fuel efficiency, reduce pollution, encourage sustainable use of natural resources, and provide for the proper care of wildlife and their natural habitats.

It would be possible for a holistic and integrative concept like the common good to become a Rousseauian tool for pressuring a minority or a group of dissenters to conform to the domination of the powerful who claim to speak for the common good. Evangelicals' and Catholics' respect for a heritage as persecuted minorities struggling for religious liberty, may make us especially aware of the danger of domination by the powerful. Therefore three themes in the encyclicals are especially important for us: (1) Tying the common good to *rights of the widows, orphans, poor, and immigrants* —the powerless—and to the outcasts excluded from community. (2) Tying the common good to *human rights for people whose rights get violated* by the powerful. (3) Tying the common good to the strong affirmation of the right of religious liberty. The evangelical development of a comprehensive doctrine of human rights in England in the first half of the seventeenth century was based on the struggle for religious liberty, especially by Anabaptists and Baptists, and then the free-church movement, many of whom were executed cruelly or imprisoned for their faith. Hence the evangelical emphasis on human rights is a key entry point for evangelicals.

The Anabaptists and Baptists and free-church members after them, insisted that Jesus made disciples by teaching, not by coercion (Matt 28:19–20). Jesus said we should let the wheat and the weeds grow simultaneously (Matt 13:24–30). Jesus called us to peacemaking rather than to the authoritarian persecution that causes most wars.[21]

Hence the Vatican II *Declaration on Religious Freedom* (*Dignitatis Humanae*) is enormously helpful to evangelicals, as is the strong Catholic emphasis on human rights—not only as rights of individuals but also as rights of churches, ethnic groups, and subsidiarities. I recommend that we tie our common theme of the common good strongly to our equally common theme of human rights, and vice versa. Everything we say about the common good in our writings could be said, point by point, about what we write about human rights.

21. *For the Health of the Nation*, 368.

12

Morality, Government, and the Common Good: Understanding How Coercive Power Operates Morally in Our Daily Lives

DANIEL FINN

INTRODUCTION

THE PHILOSOPHER THOMAS NAGEL criticized libertarian Robert Nozick for elevating "the unimpeded exercise of the will into the supreme principle of morality."[1] While Nozick is more extreme in this insistence than conservative Christian commentators on economic life, there has been a noticeable shift toward libertarian thinking among "neo-conservative" Catholics, largely out of an interest in arguing for smaller government. (This may also be occurring in evangelical Christianity, but I leave that argument to other participants in our dialogue.) While this essay cannot review the whole of that development, it will argue that this rightward movement—away from the communal notion of the common good in Catholic social thought—is rooted in a misunderstanding of the role of coercive power, particularly as exercised by government, as essential to the common good.

---

1. Thomas Nagel, *Yale Law Journal*, vol. 85, no. 1 (November 1975) 136–149, at 144.

THE COMMON GOOD

One of the more fundamental notions in Catholic social thought is the common good. The bishops of the Second Vatican Council defined it as "the sum of those conditions of social life which allow social groups and their individual members relatively thorough and ready access to their own fulfillment."[2] But perhaps the explanation of the common good that is the clearest and most adequate is provided by Virgil Michel, OSB.[3] The common good has two essential dimensions. The first encompasses the common conditions of social life. The second entails the attainment of the good life by everyone, at least to a minimum degree.

The common conditions of social life refer to those conditions that are necessary for the human person to develop and flourish, but which no one person can possibly create alone. These include social organization, peace, order, opportunities for education, work, and self-development, freedom for the higher things in life, etc. Consider personal security on the street. We know that there are places in the world—perhaps even in our own city—where it is not safe to walk the streets alone at night, or perhaps even at noon. At the same time, most of us who are economically prosperous live in neighborhoods where it is safe to walk about. How much more likely it is that a person can flourish in pursuing a meaningful life in safety than in its absence? And that condition of safety has to be "produced" by the community, not by the individual. Business executives in a Mexican city plagued by drug cartels can hire body guards and drive in bullet-proof automobiles, but they cannot thereby feel truly safe. Human flourishing requires the presence of common conditions of social life that no individual can generate.

The second dimension of the common good in Virgil Michel's definition is equally necessary: the attainment of "the good life" by all, at least to a minimum degree. Implicit here is the basic idea, affirmed by the Judeo-Christian tradition from the beginning, that a thriving society is one where everyone develops personally and has access to what is needed to flourish. There is no intention here that all incomes should be equal, since the tradition has recognized that there are good moral reasons why some may have higher income or wealth than others—as incentive for harder work, more extensive education, or greater risk, etc. But from the gleaning laws of the

2. *Gaudium et Spes*, para. 26.

3. Virgil Michel, OSB, "The Common Good," in *Christian Social Reconstruction* (Milwaukee: Bruce, 1937), 126–32.

Torah to Jesus' preaching of love of neighbor to the understanding of the obligations of property owners articulated in the early church, the middle ages, and the Reformation, the tradition has always insisted that the needs of everyone be met, in fulfillment of God's intention in the gift of the earth.

Clearly, individuals, government, and society all have roles in this generation of the common good. And in each case, there are important issues under debate today. Yet one of the most fundamental elements in communal life is widely misunderstood, if not ignored completely: power.

POWER

Daily life is laced with relationships of power. I will focus here not on all kinds of power but on what is typically called "power-over," a relationship where one person constrains the actions of another. In *Comprehending Power in Christian Social Ethics*, Christine Firer Hinze has written helpfully on Christian ethics and "power-to," where one person enables another to do something, perhaps by facilitating personal growth in the other.[4] Anna Mercedes's *Power For: Feminism and Christ's Self Giving* addresses the role of kenosis in a Christian embodiment of "power-for."[5] My focus will be on "power-over."

As Thomas Wartenberg[6] has argued, there are three kinds of power over others: force, coercion, and influence. Here we will speak largely of the second, as it is the most misunderstood, but let us consider first the character of all three.

First, force occurs when one person prevents another from doing something. We often think of the morally objectionable forms of force—when employed by a dictator or a thug on the street. But if you try to cross those yellow plastic police tapes to enter a crime scene, you'll soon be confronted by a police officer who will prevent you from going forward. Toddlers who want to wander into the street are typically picked up by their parents and placed down again on the sidewalk. And you yourself might

---

4. Christine Firer Hinze, *Comprehending Power in Christian Social Ethics* (Atlanta: Scholars, 1995).

5. Anna Mercedes, *Power For: Feminism and Christ's Self Giving* (London: T&T Clark, 2011).

6. I am indebted to Thomas Wartenberg for this analysis of power. See Wartenberg, *The Forms of Power: From Domination to Transformation* (Philadelphia: Temple University Press, 1990).

physically restrain a frantic neighbor to prevent her from re-entering her burning house in search of a missing child. Force cannot "make" anyone do anything, of course, although those subject to force must decide what to do in light of the force they encounter. And force can be either moral or immoral.

The second form of power over is coercion, which is best defined as a successful threat. Person A tells Person B that B must do X (something B doesn't want to do) or Y will happen. Person B then decides to do X. People often think of coercion as always morally objectionable, as when the mafia boss in the movies "makes an offer you cannot refuse." But coercion occurs when a university professor's syllabus states the course requirements, threatening a failing grade if they are not met. Parents often tell their teenage children: you must do this (or not do that) or you will pay a penalty. These are forms of coercion, usually quite moral.

Third, influence is a form of power when Person A, who holds coercive power over Person B, wants to convince B of some idea, even if A doesn't want the coercive power to be the reason that B accepts the idea. This is a ubiquitous problem in the college classroom (but also in parents' reasoning with their teenagers and in the Vatican's attempts to persuade dissident theologians): A wants to persuade B of the wisdom of something without coercion, but the interpersonal persuasion is deeply affected by the fact that A does simultaneously hold coercive power over B.

To return to coercion, the focus of this essay, critics of government often emphasize that relying on government to accomplish one thing or another in economic life is dangerous or simply bad because of "the coercive power of government." Markets, it is said, rely on mutual voluntary participation, but government relies on coercion. But careful thought indicates that daily life is replete with coercive relationships, often for the good of all involved.

Parents coerce their six-year-olds when they tell them that certain "logical consequences" (which the child won't like) will ensue if the child insists on screaming in the restaurant or throwing a ball at his younger sister. And each time I would prefer to drive very fast when late for an important meeting, the threat of getting a speeding ticket coerces me, for the common good.

Every club that intends to accomplish something relies on coercion: if you don't pay your dues, you will be dropped from membership. Every employee at work knows that to break the rules could lead to being fired.

Coercion is part of the software that allows daily life to boot up each morning. When institutions are well-structured, all persons involved—those who hold coercive power and those who are subject to it—understand how the system works and at its best support that system, even if they might believe there are better ways it could be structured.

In well-functioning institutions, the presence of coercive power is most of the time "in the background." It is not in the front of consciousness, not something everyone is aware of all the time. In a good work situation, employees work productively not because they might get fired but because they enjoy their work and respect their boss. In most college classrooms, the threat of a failing grade is not consciously a part of the faculty-student relationship (though it is far more frequently for students than for faculty—a fact of power relationships: that those subject to power are far more aware of it than are those wielding that power).

And the same is true for a well-governed society. At its best, citizens live out their daily lives, even their relationships with government agents like the police officer who drives by or county clerk who receives property taxes, without having in mind the most severe penalties government can impose, such as jail time. Citizens may joke about the threat of jail if they don't file their income tax returns by April 15, but life is richer and more meaningful when they do pay their taxes on time, with no more angst than accompanies the need to pay the bill for lunch at a restaurant.

Those on the political right who propose we should think of government primarily as a coercive reality in our lives rarely admit to the widespread occurrence of other coercive relationships. It's no more accurate to describe government as primarily coercive than to say the same about the relationship between parents and their children or between the classroom teacher and her students. Such reductionism eviscerates the meaning of life.

MORALITY AND THE LAW

Not only do right wing Catholic commentators misconstrue the empirical situation in thinking that coercion is unique to government action, they also are then tempted to misunderstand the moral character of that same relation to law, the coercive power of government. Too often, neo-conservative Catholics talk as if the law undercuts the moral life; in the Catholic tradition, the law supports it.

For example, Fr. Robert Sirico, president of the Acton Institute, has questioned the collection of taxes to help the poor because he believes this contribution of taxpayers cannot be part of a virtuous person's living out of the gospel. He argues that when a law requires a particular action that action loses its voluntariness, and thus its moral significance. "That we go along with the demand is no great credit to our sense of humanitarianism or charity," he writes. "The impulse here is essentially one of fear."[7] In other words, he apparently believes that a legal obligation makes virtuous behavior impossible.

But this is to misconstrue the moral life, particularly as understood in Catholic moral theology. The law cannot substitute for virtuous behavior, of course, but it does not prevent it either. Thomas Aquinas taught that virtue entails a constant will to act rightly, and that those who don't learn virtue from their parents need the "discipline of laws" to keep them "restrained from evil by force and fear." Thomas goes on to say that unvirtuous men, "by being habituated in this way, might be brought to do willingly what hitherto they did from fear, and thus become virtuous."[8] But if law can "habituate" so that even the unvirtuous evildoer might eventually act out of virtue, then surely the virtuous individual can act voluntarily and virtuously in spite of a law that would constrain him to act differently if he needed it. We might ask Fr. Sirico why it is that he does not sexually harass his female employees at the Acton Institute. Is it merely because the law forbids these behaviors? Would he really claim that the day before the state legislature made sexual harassment a crime he was acting virtuously, but a day later he was acting out of fear?

Turning to taxation to help the poor, Sirico says, "I cannot see how this method of redistributing wealth has anything to do with the Gospel." He adds that "a government program effects nothing toward fulfilling the Gospel requirement that we give of our own time and income toward assisting the poor."[9] But this would seem to be a failure to recognize that, in a democracy, government is self-government. We the people, through our representatives, have initiated programs such as Social Security for the elderly, unemployment insurance for those losing a job in a recession, and various programs to assist low-income mothers, their children, and the

---

7. Robert Sirico, *Religion and Liberty*, vol. 17, no. 4.

8. Thomas Aquinas, *Summa Theologica*, I–II, Q 95, "On Human Law," a. 1, in *The Political Ideas of St. Thomas Aquinas*, ed. Dino Bigongiari, New York: Hafner, 1953), 56.

9. Sirico, *Religion and Liberty*.

poor more generally. We do indeed have the obligation to assist the needy with our time and to give generously to private charities. That is, government programs cannot suffice to fulfill our obligations to the poor.

But the issue Sirico presses here is whether the assistance to the poor provided by democratic government can even be part of our response to the gospel. It surely is, and that is why Pope John Paul II insisted, for example, that government ensure "in every case the necessary minimum support for the unemployed worker."[10] Similarly, Pope Benedict XVI certainly understood the role of the state in Catholic social thought when he warned against "abandoning mechanisms of wealth redistribution."[11]

CONCLUSION

In summary, the Catholic understanding of the common good requires that all persons achieve "the good life" at least to a minimum degree. And this requires the common conditions of social life that are generated by the community—both by society (the many organizations of civil society) and by government (the institution by which, in a democracy, we govern ourselves). It is no surprise that government relies on coercive power, since those in authority in nearly every other organization do as well, from parents to teachers to employers to club presidents. Coercion is neither always good nor always bad. The key is that it be exercised morally.

10. Pope John Paul II, *Centesimus Annus*, para. 15.

11. Pope Benedict XVI, *Caritas in Veritate*, para. 32.

13

A Vision for Major, Sustained Catholic-Evangelical Partnership on Public Policy

Ronald J. Sider

WELL BEFORE INDIVIDUALS STARTED pointing out the striking similarity of official Catholic teaching on public policy and that of the National Association of Evangelicals (as represented by their unanimously approved *For the Health of the Nation: An Evangelical Call to Civic Responsibility*), I had frequently reflected on how parallel to Catholic social teaching were the political views of a growing evangelical center. I was, therefore, very pleased when private conversations led to the discussion to have an exploratory dialogue on the topic in March 2006 at Georgetown University.

At our second meeting (April 24–26, 2008), I sketched very briefly a rather broad (some might say grandiose!) vision for a large, sustained, cooperative effort. It is obvious, more than eight years later, that our annual stimulating three-day dialogues have not led to the large cooperative effort that I hoped for in 2008. But I still think the kind of ambitious, decades-long cooperative effort I proposed would be wise and significant. I will therefore, start with my original proposals presented in 2008 and then offer some current reflections.

1. THE VISION

Statements by American Catholic Bishops and the Vatican's *Compendium of the Church's Social Teaching* on the one hand and the National Association of Evangelicals' *For the Health of the Nation: An Evangelical Call to Civic Responsibility*[1] on the other reflect enormous common ground. The areas of disagreement are minor and few. Both documents reflect what some have called the "seamless garment," or a "completely/consistently pro-life" stance or a "biblically balanced agenda." It is clearly pro-life *and* pro-poor, pro-family *and* pro-racial justice, pro-peacemaking *and* pro-creation care.

I believe that it is possible for large numbers of Catholics and Evangelicals to develop processes, strategies, and structures to work much more closely together on this common agenda in the next two decades. (Large numbers of African Americans and Latinos are also strongly pro-life and pro-family and would gladly join a movement that was also working hard for racial and economic justice.) White evangelicals and Catholics make up half of all voters. If one adds the non-Catholic African American and non-Catholic Latino communities, one adds another 10–15 percent of all voters. If only a substantial minority of these communities developed a sustained, sophisticated, comprehensive cooperative effort to reshape American culture and politics on the basis of this shared common agenda, we could change American life in profound ways.

There has been significant discussion of evangelical-Catholic relationships in recent years. One thinks for example of William M. Shea's *The Lion and the Lamb: Evangelicals and Catholics in America* (Oxford, 2004) or Mark Noll and Carolyn Nystrom's *Is the Reformation Over?* (Baker, 2005). In 2007, InterVarsity Press published a major volume in which evangelical scholars responded (overwhelmingly positively) to the encyclicals of John Paul II (Tim Perry, ed., *The Legacy of John Paul II*).

I find it significant that Cardinal Edward Cassidy, as president of the Pontifical Council for Promoting Christian Unity, called for this kind of cooperation. In a chapter in *Catholics and Evangelicals* edited by Thomas P. Raush (Paulist, 2000), Cardinal Cassidy noted that "these two Christian communities remain far apart in respect to their doctrinal understanding . . . Yet at the same time they often find themselves sharing a common approach to ethical questions and to other matters relating to the public forum." Catholics and Evangelicals, he said:

> share a similar vision on many questions concerning life and morals. As they cross together the threshold of a new Christian Millennium, Catholics and Evangelicals will be challenged with many

1. See Ronald J. Sider and Diane Knippers, eds., *Toward An Evangelical Public Policy* (Grand Rapids: Baker, 2005), 363–75.

identical problems. Their primary concern will be how to define and promote fundamental Christian values in an ever more pluralistic, secularized society deeply influenced by neo-liberalism and unbridled consumerism. Surely this challenge should urge these two communities to rid themselves of all misunderstandings, stereotypes and myths about the other and encourage them to join their powerful forces in a common struggle to conserve their Christian heritage and its fundamental values. This seems to me to be a service to the world of the twenty-first century, to which they are called by the Lord himself (174–75).

I agree strongly with Cardinal Cassidy's call for Roman Catholics and evangelicals to work together on questions of public life. And I think that should be easier than even he suggests because I think he overstates the doctrinal differences. It is certainly true that there are major theological differences between Catholics and evangelicals (e.g. the Eucharist, papal authority, tradition, the role of Mary, etc.). But the common ground shared by Catholics and evangelicals is even more striking. We both confess that God is Father, Son, and Holy Spirit; that Jesus Christ is true God and true man; that Jesus is the only way to salvation; that Jesus rose bodily from the dead on the third day; and that the Bible is God's reliable, authoritative, unique revelation. That represents a vast amount of common ground that provides a strong foundation for cooperation in shaping culture and public life.

At the first meeting of this group in March 2006, we agreed in a final statement that we should work together on the common agenda of the two documents mentioned earlier.

In the now famous document, "Evangelicals and Catholics Together," Richard John Neuhaus, Charles Colson, and their colleagues also called for this kind of cooperation. I believe "Evangelicals and Catholics Together" is enormously important and largely correct in what it calls for. Unfortunately, the social agenda spelled out for common action tends largely to represent conservative issues. There is very little in the document on justice for the poor, environmental issues, or racism.

I believe that if our two communities are to work together in a way that effects lasting substantial change, we must work together on the whole agenda we have in common, not just part of it. The statements of the Catholic magisterium and the NAE offer the right comprehensive agenda. It would be silly to develop a "progressive" alternative to Neuhaus/Colson. What we need is a major new Evangelical/Catholic cooperative movement that brings together the major voices of both communities. That means that the center of both communities should take the lead but also that major representative voices of both evangelical and Catholic "conservatives" and "progressives" must also be engaged—as long as we all together embrace the full agenda of our respective communities as represented in the documents mentioned above.

How do we do that? I want to sketch the outline of such a sustained, comprehensive cooperative effort. I ask: What are all the things we would need to do to engage in that kind of successful movement in the next twenty years?

I believe that we would need teams of our best activists/practitioners and scholars from evangelical and Catholic colleges and universities working together on a vast range of issues. Teams of scholars/activists could function as think tanks. We would need cooperative strategies to permeate the broader culture (the arts, education, etc.) and public policy with our ideas. We would need both long-term and shorter-term strategies to shape culture and public life.

We would need teams of scholars/activists working in at least five basic areas: 1) foundational theological, philosophical issues; 2) a comprehensive conceptual framework for our "seamless garment," "completely pro-life" vision; 3) a twenty-year plan; 4) ten-year plans; 5) four-year plans. In each case we would need work both on the overall, integrated vision and specific work on the approximately seven to ten areas where we would concentrate (sanctity of human life; economic justice; family; religious freedom; creation care/environment; peacemaking; human rights; racial and gender justice). We would also need different teams working on the broad shaping of the culture on the one hand and the more narrow task of shaping public policy on the other.

2. FUNDAMENTAL THEOLOGICAL/PHILOSOPHICAL ISSUES.

We need more careful deliberation to discover and define the precise issues needing work. But some basic issues are clear: (a) the interrelationship between natural law, tradition, church authority, and biblical revelation as the foundations for our normative framework; (b) the role of government. Currently, evangelicals tend to be more skeptical of the role of government than do Catholics.

As we worked together, we would undoubtedly identify both additional broad foundational issues that relate to our common agenda as well as more specific foundational issues that relate to one or another of our seven to ten specific areas.

3. A TWENTY-YEAR VISION.

We ought to have teams of activists/scholars developing a vision for where we want to be in twenty years and how we can together shape the culture and public life over two decades to accomplish that.

Some teams would focus largely on shaping culture, others largely on impacting public policy. Here as elsewhere, there would need to be teams focused on the overall seamless garment agenda and others focused on each of the specific issues.

4. TEN-YEAR PLANS.

The various teams described above would develop more detailed plans and agendas for shaping culture and public policy over the next ten years.

5. FOUR-YEAR PLANS.

Teams would also need to develop even more detailed agendas for cooperation with a focus on the next presidential election. These teams would formulate very specific goals and strategies (e.g., very concrete agendas for elected officials such as embracing the goal of reducing poverty and abortion by fifty percent in the next ten years, etc.).

6. IMPLEMENTATION.

If we are to accomplish anything like the above, we will need a clearly defined governing structure, substantial funding, executive implementation, and regular meetings.

The present committee of evangelicals and Catholics could be expanded appropriately for proper balance and serve as the governing body shaping the overall process.

An executive group to implement the activities would be needed in each community—perhaps a center at both Georgetown University and Eastern University.

Obviously, major funding would be needed. If the process developed substantial prominence, many scholars and activists would gladly donate time to work on the many teams needed. But there would be a growing need for funds for the two executive groups, for travel for team members, meetings, etc. To the extent that the vision and activities of this cooperative project caught the vision of both communities, increasing sources of funding would become available.

At least once a year a several-day meeting would be important: to hear and debate reports from various teams; to make major decisions; to celebrate, pray, fellowship, and worship together.

In all probability, the work of many teams would be published in books and popularized in booklets and articles.

That was my proposal in 2008. Today, I still think the basic assumptions (widespread official agreement on matters of public policy and a potentially large block of voters that could share that broad agenda) are correct. I also think it is even more clear today that American society desperately needs that kind of sustained voice.

It is obvious, of course, that our annual meetings did not lead to anything like what I had proposed. We have had wonderful, stimulating conversation and have come to understand and appreciate each other better. We agreed in 2010 to try to foster regional dialogue centered on more local groups of evangelical and Catholic colleges/universities. Only one happened.

So why has so little happened?

For one thing, we are too busy. All the people involved are busy scholars and/or activists with important institutional responsibilities. (John Carr, long-time head of the US Catholic Bishops' public policy work likes to joke that one of his responsibilities in life is to say "no" to my grandiose proposals!) None of us found the time to raise the money and develop the structures to test the idea of a much larger, sustained cooperative effort. (Whether the financial resources would really be there if a well-organized effort were actually launched is an open question.)

Second, we never achieved the active participation of the full range of voices in each community that I originally hoped for. There are, as everyone knows, major differences within both the Catholic and evangelical communities on the best concrete political steps to take to implement the completely pro-life agenda officially endorsed by both communities. For my vision to have succeeded, we would have needed more "buy-in" by the full range of centrists, conservatives, and progressives. Finally, it is a fundamental violation of the unity of the one body of Christ not to bring together the "conservative" and "liberal" members of our communities to seek substantial agreement. But we had only very limited success in this area.

Third, precisely because a "completely pro-life" agenda is not welcomed (often not even tolerated) in either major political party, actually making progress on that whole agenda is complicated. Party affiliation and regular political seasons (House, Senate, and presidential elections) complicate the efforts of pro-life *and* pro-poor, pro-family, *and* pro-peace and creation-care movements. A sustained effort on this broad agenda would need to discover better ways to deal with these pressures and respond to the charges that promoting this whole agenda undermines this or that specific issue that some consider all-important. It would also have to somehow successfully deal with the fact that the political climate has become increasingly divisive, harsh, and uncivil.

Fourth, neither community has been very successful in persuading a majority of its people to vigorously press for the full "completely pro-life" agenda endorsed by both sets of leaders. As the 2016 elections demonstrated so clearly, large numbers of Catholic and evangelical voters simply ignore their church leaders' call to embrace a "completely pro-life" agenda. Any successful, sustained, cooperative movement of Catholics and evangelicals on that whole agenda would have to devote massive energy to persuading more people in both communities to embrace what their leaders teach.

I do not think that our conversations uncovered any substantial, foundational disagreements that would in principle make major, sustained Catholic-evangelical cooperation highly problematic. We knew from the beginning that Catholics place more emphasis on natural law as their foundation for public policy than do evangelicals. But our conversations did not show that evangelicals' greater reliance on Scripture would place significant barriers in the way of cooperation on concrete agendas. Similarly, we also knew from the beginning that at the popular level, evangelicals tend to be more suspicious of governmental solutions to societal problems than are Catholics. But I have not found any foundational reasons in evangelical theology that require anything approaching a libertarian view of government even though significant numbers of evangelicals do, at the popular level, lean in that direction. Our several years of dialogue did not identify any substantial foundational theological/philosophical barriers to greater cooperation.

In light of the desperate challenges in our nation and world (widespread poverty and economic injustice, growing threats to the sanctity of human life, devastation in our families, an increasing willingness to abandon the understanding of marriage embraced by virtually all civilizations for millennia, and increasingly likely colossal environmental calamities), it seems unthinkable to me that Catholics and evangelicals would fail to seize the opportunity to work together on their common agenda. In the face of such daunting challenges, it would seem to be the height of irresponsibility not to launch a massive effort to work together on our shared agenda.

I do not know how—concretely and effectively—to do that. Many of our colleges and universities have their own public policy centers. Perhaps we could develop some network of those centers that would facilitate dialogue, cooperation, and integrated effort. We certainly need new programs with better techniques to educate and mobilize the laity in both communities so that millions more Catholic and evangelical laity truly embrace what their leaders teach. But I do not pretend to have a master plan or the funding to do what I hope and pray will happen.

So I end where I began when we first started. I think the kind of large, sustained cooperation of the kind I suggested is still possible. I think our society needs it now more than ever. Please God, may some younger, wiser Catholic and evangelical leaders figure out how to do it.